J. HARVIE WILKINSON, JR.

J. HARVIE WILKINSON, JR.

Virginian, Banker, Visionary

by WILLIAM K. KLINGAMAN

Published by Crestar Financial Corporation
Designed by Raymond Geary & Associates, Richmond, Virginia
Printed by Sterling Printers, Richmond, Virginia

Library of Congress Catalog Card Number: 94-079140
ISBN 0-9643605-0-0

CONTENTS

ACKNOWLEDGMENTS

This has been one of the most enjoyable projects I have ever worked on, partly because the subject was so fascinating, but also because the people I have had the pleasure of working with have been absolutely delightful. I would like to take this opportunity to thank everyone involved, particularly Letitia Wilkinson, J. Harvie Wilkinson III, and Lewis Wilkinson, who generously shared their family memories and made me feel like a member of the Wilkinson family myself. Besides sharing his own recollections with me, Richard Dilworth graciously agreed to review the manuscript. Richard Tilghman, the chairman and chief executive officer of Crestar was kind enough to provide his personal support throughout the project. This biography would never have seen the light of day, however, without the steadfast assistance of Marion George, who guided me through innumerable crises and coordinated the project from start to finish.

I would also like to thank all the individuals who consented to share their memories of Harvie Wilkinson with me: Justice Lewis Powell, Governor Mills Godwin, Edgar Shannon, Paul Sackett, Jack Jennings, Lewis Flinn, Mary Page Winberg, Virginius Dabney, Jim Rawles, Jim Wilson, Jack McElroy, Tennant Bryan, Joe Carter, Bob Buford, Frank Fagan, Gordon Davies, Harvie Fitzgerald, Tom Jarman, William Higgins, Lee Switz, Lloyd Noland, Paul Douglas, Joe Cullman, Chuck Longsworth, Claiborne Robins and Paul Funkhouser. I wish all of them the best, and hope that they enjoy this volume. Any errors that remain in the book are, of course, my responsibility.

—W. K. K.

September, 1994

INTRODUCTION

The story of Harvie Wilkinson presented in this book is more than the story of one businessman's career. It is the story of how an individual with extraordinary vision and drive created not only an institution — today's Crestar Financial Corporation — but also shaped the structure of the entire banking industry in the Commonwealth of Virginia.

Equally important, the author documents what a profound and positive impact Harvie had on his community over the course of six decades, giving generously of his time and talent to improve the funding and quality of public education in Virginia, to effect innovation and change in government and to promote many worthwhile charitable and cultural organizations.

Harvie's broad knowledge of business and public affairs, coupled with unerringly accurate judgement and a unique ability to balance wisdom with wit, set the standard against which leaders in industry — indeed leaders in general — might well be judged today. I don't think it an exaggeration to suggest that few would measure up.

In his forty-plus years with the bank, Harvie consciously endeavored to continue his education and expand his knowledge of the banking industry he loved as well as the world in general, and by extension, the bank and his associates benefited from his efforts. His desire to excel and expand his accomplishments inspired us and we endeavored in our own individual ways to emulate him. His enthusiasm for his work and dedication to his family, friends and community were contagious.

Those who had the opportunity to know and work firsthand with Harvie were fortunate. Through this book, I hope others can benefit as well.

Richard G. Tilghman
Chairman, Crestar Financial Corporation

October, 1994

I

FROM RICHMOND TO NEW YORK

In the South we tend to look at our roots.
Should we not look at the stars?

— J. HARVIE WILKINSON, JR.

In the early 1930s, four close friends gathered frequently for lunch at the Occidental Restaurant in downtown Richmond, Virginia. It was a remarkably talented group, though at the time few people outside the city would have recognized any of their names. Two members of this party — George Gibson and Lewis F. Powell, Jr. — were attorneys; a third, Virginius Dabney, was a journalist, while the fourth was a bank executive named J. Harvie Wilkinson, Jr. Like many young professionals at the outset of their careers, these men each possessed ambitious dreams and plans for themselves, for their city, and for their native Commonwealth of Virginia.

During the ensuing decades, all four of these gentlemen would achieve extraordinary success in their chosen fields, perhaps surpassing even the visions they dared to share with one another in those youthful days. Certainly the history of Virginia would have been far different, and far poorer for the absence of any of them. Both Gibson and Powell went on to enjoy distinguished legal careers, with Powell capping a life in the law by becoming the first Virginian to sit on the Supreme Court of the United States in more than a century. V. Dabney, the sparkling literary talent of the group, served as editor of the city's leading newspaper, the *Richmond Times-Dispatch*, for thirty-three years, and won a Pulitzer Prize for his editorial writing. And Harvie Wilkinson, the only one of the four to pursue a business career, went on to become one of twentieth-century Virginia's foremost financial executives, the head of United Virginia Bankshares, and the man who, more than any other individual, helped lead the economy of the Commonwealth into the modern era and provide it with the foundations necessary for its present prosperity. Indeed, the life and accomplishments of James Harvie Wilkinson, Jr., were so intimately intertwined with the fortunes of both Richmond and Virginia that it is difficult to imagine him as the heir of any other tradition.

His father, James Harvie Wilkinson, had been born in Virginia in the second year of the Civil War, and had grown up with two brothers on the Wilkinson family farm known as Glendale, in Powhatan County, about twenty-five miles west of Richmond. While he was still in his teens, James Wilkinson left home for life as a sailor on the merchant vessels that plied the Kanawha Canal, then one of the major commercial arteries between the state capital and the western Virginia city of Lynchburg.

Although he subsequently became captain of a canal boat, Wilkinson decided that the future looked considerably more promising in selling than in moving goods, and so he left the canal and went to work for several of his uncles who owned a Richmond dry goods firm known as Anderson, Epes, and Cardozo. (The family connection stemmed from the Cardozo line. James Harvie Wilkinson's mother's maiden name was Emily Cardozo, and through that line there would be a family connection between Harvie Wilkinson and Benjamin Cardozo, the prominent U.S. Supreme Court Justice of the early twentieth century.)

In those years — as for most of its history — Richmond was an excellent location for a wholesale dry goods business, because the city's railway and water transportation connections made it a primary distribution center for merchants throughout much of the upper South, from South Carolina to West Virginia. Indeed, the site of the city had originally been chosen for settlement because ocean-going vessels sailing up the James River could proceed as far as its docks, but no further.

After learning as much as he could about the wholesale business from his uncles, Captain Wilkinson left to embark upon his own commercial enterprise. On December 18, 1893, at the age of thirty-one, he married a former elocution teacher, Neilie McCurdy Smith, a gentle but strong-minded woman who was the daughter of a local tobacco merchant. Their first child, Marie Mosby Wilkinson, was born in 1900, and

Harvie's father, James Harvie Wilkinson

by the time their second child and only son entered the world on April 14, 1906, Captain Wilkinson had become senior partner of Richmond's leading wholesale dry goods and notions firm — Wilkinson, Williams, and Reed, Inc., located at 1413-1417 East Franklin Street in the city's downtown business district.

Like his father, the boy — who was born in the family's home at 313 North Harrison Street — bore the middle name of Harvie, the surname of a doctor who had once saved Captain Wilkinson's father from drowning. But it was not at all certain that young James Harvie Wilkinson, Jr. would ever live to see his first birthday. He was so small and frail at birth that the doctors feared for his life. The attending physician at the delivery strongly urged his parents to take the infant to the country for an extended stay, so he could receive the salutary effects of fresh air. To Captain Wilkinson, meanwhile, the doctor confided that "I cannot promise you that the chances are good that he will come back alive."

James Wilkinson (fourth from right), in front of one of his early wholesale notions businesses, located at 1209 East Main Street in Richmond.

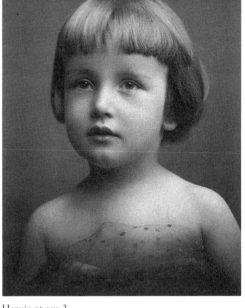

Harvie with his proud parents.   Harvie at age 3.

But Harvie Junior, as his mother called him, did return with his parents to Richmond, bearing no trace of illness, though he was usually one of the smaller children in his neighborhood along Harrison Street, in the city's historic Fan District. To keep up with the other boys, Harvie had to develop a considerable measure of pluck and perseverance. There is a story that Harvie and several older boys were once engaged in a game of spies and armies, and that Harvie was stationed as a lookout behind a barrel at a strategic corner of the neighborhood. As twilight fell and the rest of the gang returned to their homes, Harvie's parents grew concerned over their son's continued absence. Finally one of Harvie's playmates remembered that they had given Harvie orders to remain at his post until he was relieved, and that was precisely where his parents found him, still dutifully hiding behind the barrel and keeping watch for "the enemy."

It was Harvie's good fortune to spend the early years of his youth in a city that was prosperous and constantly expanding its horizons, with the outward scars of the Civil War finally healing. By 1910, when Harvie was four years old, the population of

Richmond's Broad Street about 1910 at the corner of
Sixth Street, with Miller & Rhoads at right.

Richmond had risen to 127,000, including the residents of the town of Manchester to the
south, which had recently been incorporated into the city limits. Although Virginia's
economy remained primarily agricultural, with tobacco as the foremost crop, Richmond
had become the second leading industrial center in the South (behind only Louisville),
boasting nearly 1,500 manufacturing plants with a total of 31,000 workers. And as the
nation recovered from the devastating financial panic of 1907, commercial activity in
and around Richmond began to boom, with three railroads — the Chesapeake & Ohio,
Southern Railway, and the Seaboard Air Line (on which one reportedly rode "as light as
air" on the rails) — employing the city as a terminus.

Progress certainly appeared to be the order of the day. Throughout the old
residential neighborhoods, stately antebellum mansions were being torn down to make
way for new dwellings or office buildings. The first generation of automobiles — there
were still only 140,000 in the entire country at that time — was wending its way carefully
through the streets of Richmond, bound perhaps for the fashionable shops along the

The 700 block of Broad Street with Hellstern's Drug
Store at far right.

southern side of Broad Street (the northern side was reserved for saloons and other
similarly disreputable establishments), or perhaps the financial district on Main Street
(assuming that the James River had not flooded the lower end of town yet again).

Richmond in those years was a relatively compact city, with about 95 percent of
its population residing east of the Boulevard. Motorists venturing outside the city limits
did so at their peril, for the roads outside of town could quickly turn into quagmires,
providing local farmers with an opportunity to supplement their income by using their
teams to pull stalled autos out of muddy ditches. Less adventurous travelers could ride the
city's streetcars — which, in the summertime, were open cars with long wooden
benches — for a nickel, though this mode of transportation often carried an additional
cost in sheer frustration. As Lewis Powell once pointed out, the streetcars "never went as
fast as you wanted them to, and they were usually late."

Those searching for an evening's entertainment could choose from among the
thirty theaters that graced Richmond, offering fare that varied from vaudeville to

Broadway shows. If none of those options pleased, there were usually concerts at the Municipal Auditorium, and a selection of silent films at the city's new motion picture houses. After the show, men in their straw hats and seersucker suits and ladies in their gored skirts and shirtwaists with leg-of-mutton sleeves could meet at T. A. Miller's drugstore for a claret limeade, or an ice cream soda at Hellstern's, near the corner of Seventh and Broad. Well-bred women in those days wore little or no makeup, however; such artifices were reserved for the ladies of the evening who plied their trade — legally — on Mayo Street.

If Richmond provided a wealth of cultural and economic opportunities at the turn of the century, the city had less reason to be proud of its system of public education. Like most of the nation, Richmond had never needed many secondary schools, since most children in nineteenth-century America simply went to work on the farm or in the factory after completing grammar school. Still, the single high school within the city limits in 1906 — Richmond High School — was clearly in need of greater attention, suffering from an inadequate physical plant and insufficient maintenance. The opening of John Marshall High School several years later eased conditions significantly, and yet most Richmond parents continued to send their children to private schools if they could bear the cost of tuition.

That was the course young Harvie Wilkinson's parents chose for him. Mr. Wilkinson had always been an extremely well-read man, whose library contained all the classics of English literature, from the works of Shakespeare to Thackeray and Sir Walter Scott. So it was not surprising that both he and Mrs. Wilkinson took a keen interest in their son's education. First came two years of preparatory schooling at the Scott Talcott School, a private educational institution located on Lombardy Street in Richmond's Fan District, and led by headmistress Miss Hallie Talcott. Then, in 1915, Harvie's father had to decide whether to send Harvie to the recently-established Chamberlayne School for Boys, (which was subsequently purchased by the Episcopal Diocese and renamed St. Christopher's), the Richmond Academy, or the McGuire University School. While all three schools enjoyed excellent reputations, Captain Wilkinson chose the latter, much to the enthusiastic delight of his son. Years later, Harvie Wilkinson would recall his years at the McGuire School as among the happiest and proudest moments of his life. It was there he first met Lewis F. Powell, Jr. and formed

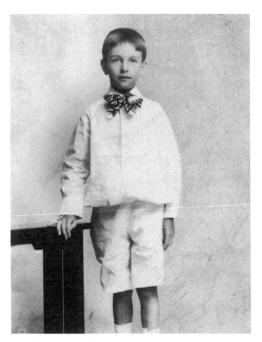

Harvie at 8 years of age.

Harvie during his last year at McGuire's University School.

a friendship that would continue to grow closer with every passing year, and it was at McGuire's that Harvie received the education in both academics and personal values that formed the cornerstone for the rest of his life.

      Much of the credit for the McGuire School's lasting impact upon its students must be given to headmaster John Peyton McGuire III, an immensely impressive gentleman, scholar, and inspiring educator who bore more than a passing physical resemblance to the much-beloved General Robert E. Lee. One writer once claimed that McGuire looked like he had stepped right out of the pages of the novel, *Gone With the Wind*. The McGuire School, founded by Lt. John Peyton McGuire Jr. of the Confederate Navy, had first opened its doors in September 1865, just a few months after the close of the war. Lt. McGuire himself led the school for the first four decades of its existence until his death in 1906, at which time his son — who already had been teaching at the school for twelve years — took over the reins.

McGuire's was, as Harvie Wilkinson later explained, "one of the last great headmaster's schools. You were conscious of being in a very remarkable place." Democratic rather than exclusive, the school admitted qualified students even if they could not afford to pay tuition; Mr. McGuire simply granted them scholarships which actually came out of his own pocket. Although the eight members of the faculty bestowed upon their charges a rigorous training in the intellectual disciplines of English, history, Latin, French, Spanish, and mathematics, it was John Peyton's intense emphasis upon an antebellum Southern sense of honor that most deeply influenced his students.

Although a certain measure of youthful high-jinks were tolerated at times, students at the McGuire School were generally expected to obey a code of behavior based upon the honor system at the University of Virginia. Indeed, the entire school operated on the premise that "all of the boys are trusted absolutely, and treated as gentlemen." For instance, when Mr. McGuire was personally teaching students in the upper classes, he would award only minor penalties (such as walking a mile in the afternoon) for such infractions as shooting spitballs or throwing erasers — so long as he was in the room when it happened. But if he left the room, the boys fell completely silent, for it was considered dishonorable to commit any infractions behind the headmaster's back. Years after they left the school, Mr. McGuire's alumni claimed that they could still recall his heartfelt talks on "honor;" indeed, many could even remember the way the word sounded when he spoke it. With deep affection and respect, Harvie Wilkinson later observed that "of all the men in Richmond in his time, he certainly has exercised the most pervasive influence right up to today."

At the time Harvie Wilkinson enrolled, the McGuire School was located at Belvedere and Main, opposite Monroe Park. Two years later, it moved to more spacious quarters in a brick building on Idlewood Avenue, overlooking Byrd Park. Even before he began his formal studies, Harvie had been taught to read by his mother, who doubtless also instructed him in elocution as well. In fact, his parents, and particularly his father, seem to have formed rather high academic expectations for Harvie Junior, as he later would for himself. Yet once his education had begun, Harvie realized that he would have to apply himself diligently to his schoolwork if he were to surpass his classmates. "I knew I was not as bright," he confided years later, "but I knew I could outwork them."

McGuire's University School building (1914-1942), opposite William Byrd Park on Idlewood Avenue in Richmond.

John Peyton McGuire III, headmaster of McGuire's University School (1906-1942).

Top: Glendale in Powhatan County, where young Harvie spent his summers.

Bottom: Harvie and his dog, Old Rambler. Harvie, learning to ride with a friend at Glendale.

And for the most part he succeeded, though not without an occasional slip. One spring morning Harvie and his father were walking to the streetcar stop together, where Mr. Wilkinson would catch a car going downtown, and Harvie would board one heading toward the McGuire School. As they neared the stop, Mr. Wilkinson — in his usual direct fashion — observed drily that "Your grades, son, are not what they should be." (Although the relationship between father and son was always cordial, it was also somewhat formal, perhaps because Wilkinson was a rather austere man, not without humor, but already 43 years old when Harvie was born.) "Yes, father," replied Harvie, "I think you're right." "Son," his father went on, "I suspect that you're thinking too much about the girls." And then he added, rather ominously, "You know which one you must choose." "Yes sir," Harvie nodded. And since, as Harvie later recalled, "those were the days that when your father said something, you did it," his grades subsequently took a decided turn for the better.

Ironically, in view of his later career as a banker, one area of study which Harvie found particularly difficult was arithmetic. He had always loved literature and Latin, but for some reason math simply did not come easily. After performing poorly on one examination, Harvie went to Mr. McGuire in deep despair, feeling that he had failed to live up to his parents' expectations. Typically, the headmaster did not lecture Harvie. Instead, he offered the young man sympathy and encouragement. "Son, don't worry," he told Harvie. "I failed that same arithmetic book, and I am Headmaster of the school. You just keep along, and you will come out all right." Heeding Mr. McGuire's advice, Harvie redoubled his academic efforts, and soon started to win ribbons for improvement in one subject after another, and eventually math became his favorite subject.

Summers were reserved for extended vacations at Glendale, the Wilkinson farm in Powhatan, with aunts and uncles, and games with neighboring children, and the love of the favorite family dog, a hound known as "Old Rambler," who once had the embarrassing misfortune to be nearly drowned by a raccoon. At Glendale, Harvie — who was nicknamed "Little Captain" because of his father's former occupation — was given a plot of land to tend on his own. Usually he raised a crop of tobacco on it. "Uncle Claude would plant it for me," Harvie remembered, "and it was my responsibility to cultivate it, and do what is called 'suckering.' There were certain twigs that grew on the tobacco plant, and if not removed two or three times during the summer would sap the strength of the plant. Plowing between the rows was not an easy task, but one which I found rewarding when I was given some of the proceeds from the sale of tobacco in the fall, when I returned to school." Such was the prosaic start of a singular business career.

As he grew into adolescence, Harvie began to be increasingly attracted to the prospects of a career in the world of commerce. Any hopes Harvie may have had of following in his father's footsteps and inheriting a share in the firm of Wilkinson, Williams, and Reed were dashed, however, when his father decided to sell his part of the business. Before he proceeded with the sale, Mr. Wilkinson called Harvie — who was then in his early teens — into his office and explained to him that even though the business was still profitable, and that he would like nothing better than to have Harvie succeed him in the company, he believed that the rise of chain stores and nationwide catalogue and mail-order retailers such as Sears, Roebuck and Co. would render the future of wholesaling firms uncertain at best.

Clearly the elder Wilkinson was convinced that this course would provide the best future for his son, and yet he considered it very important to make certain that Harvie understood the reasons behind it. Besides, he wished to give his son a chance to voice any objections he had to the proposed sale. Harvie replied that he was certain that his father was correct, but the discussion — and the respect his father had demonstrated for Harvie's opinions — made an indelible impression on the young man. He also may have learned a valuable lesson in business strategy by observing his father's tactics in negotiating the sale of the firm. To "put the company in play," as a later generation of financiers would put it, Wilkinson initially proposed to buy his partners out, but for an amount that was slightly less than optimal. They responded as he had hoped, making a counteroffer to purchase his interest, which he promptly accepted.

Back in school, meanwhile, Harvie's grades continued to improve. There were, of course, occasional high jinks, such as the annual Thanksgiving tradition known as "Turkey Day," when about a dozen of the older boys — known collectively as "the Turkey Committee" — would collect a quarter from each student and then assemble at the downtown markets, where they would purchase a small menagerie of ducks and turkeys. After parading around town with the fowls draped in the McGuire School's colors, the boys headed for the nearby Collegiate School for Girls to give a few rousing cheers before returning to their own school. With a great flourish of trumpets and

Harvie (front row, center) and his colleagues on the
McGuire's School "Turkey Committee." In 1923,
Harvie served as the Committee's speaker.

cackling of fowls, they burst in upon Mr. McGuire in his office and presented him with
the turkeys as a holiday gift. "He always acted as if he had never been so surprised in all
his life," Harvie recalled, "although it happened every year."

Even though he had dedicated himself assiduously to his studies, Harvie apparently did not neglect the ladies altogether in his later years at school, for the 1923 edition
of the McGuire's School Annual noted that "Harvie is exceedingly well known by all the
boys in school as a very illustrious 'lady killer.' They say he has proposed to every young
lady in town, and is now starting all over again. Nevertheless, he is a remarkably good
student for he always pulls down the royal purple."

The capstone of Harvie's career at the McGuire School came in his senior
year, when he was named the recipient of the school's most distinguished honor, the
Jack Gordon Memorial Medal. This honor, which consisted of a gold medal and a tuition
scholarship for one session, was founded in 1907 in memory of Jack Gordon, a former
McGuire's pupil and son of Colonel John W. Gordon. The boy had lost his life in a

The Jack Gordon Medal, awarded to Harvie in 1923.

gallant attempt to save a girl from drowning. Because McGuire's valued strength of character — integrity, discipline, and hard work — as well as intellectual achievement, the Jack Gordon Medal could not be won solely on academic grounds, nor for athletic accomplishments alone. Instead, it was awarded to the student who, in Mr. McGuire's estimation, had contributed the most to the school. It was a singular honor, and one which Harvie Wilkinson cherished for the rest of his life. "I think that Jack Gordon Medal meant as much to Dad as anything he ever received," noted Jay Wilkinson, Harvie's elder son. "It was the culmination of a long path of progress, and the culmination of his boyhood in many respects, because it meant that he had succeeded magnificently in the eyes of this man he respected so much."

As its name implied, the McGuire University School strove to prepare its students for further studies at the University of Virginia, Mr. McGuire's alma mater. Unlike other schools, however, McGuire's never gave its graduates diplomas, nor did it hold commencement exercises. Instead, Mr. McGuire simply informed his students when

Harvie, with his bags packed, ready to depart for the
University of Virginia.

it was time, in his judgment, for them to proceed to the next level in their education.
Most of McGuire's students, of course, went on to the University of Virginia in
Charlottesville, though there were occasional exceptions (including — much to
Mr. McGuire's dismay — Lewis F. Powell, Jr., who elected to enroll instead at
Washington and Lee on a baseball scholarship).

In the autumn of 1923, Harvie headed west to Charlottesville, the first member
of his family ever to enroll at the University of Virginia. (His sister, Marie, who was also
an excellent student, had wanted to attend Columbia University, but at that time it was
still rare for southern women to further their education at a university. And if a family
had limited financial resources, it was traditionally the son who received the first
opportunity to continue his studies.)

When he began his freshman year, Harvie intended to major in chemical
engineering, one of the "high-technology" fields of study of that era which appeared to
hold the promise of substantial growth in the coming decades. All those plans were

knocked into a cocked hat during his very first semester, however, when Harvie received a grade of 71 in his introductory chemistry course. It would be the only course in which he earned a grade lower than 90 during his entire college career, but it certainly was a sufficient shock to send him looking for a different career option.

He found it with the sort of clarity and certainty that comprised an almost mystical experience. It came to him suddenly and unexpectedly one evening — in his words, "like a beam of light" — after a particularly inspiring lecture by his favorite professor, Dr. E. A. Kincaid, that led him to immerse himself in volume after volume on the topic of finance. Finance...Banking...Investments. It was at that moment that Harvie understood that banking was truly the center of commerce, the hub of the business world, the locus of capital, the source of the loans and investments that drove the economy forward and generated industrial and commercial progress. "If one wants in a literal sense to be in the hub of things," Harvie once wrote, "if one likes infinite variety, if one has either a liking for detail or an appreciation of the indispensability of detail; if one realizes the value of hard facts; if one likes challenge and responsibility; if one wants a competitive environment; then he can find it in banking."

For a young man tremendously excited by the possibilities of finance, investment banking represented a fascinating opportunity to deal with not just one single company, but a wide range of enterprises, all of which depended on banks for their lifeblood of capital. In later years, Harvie Wilkinson would look back and consider himself extremely fortunate to have discovered his true calling at such an early age. "I was blessed," he said, "because so many people don't know what it is they want to do. I learned, and I was lucky." He felt such a debt of gratitude, in fact, that throughout his life he would always take time and special care to advise young people who came to him for suggestions on how to find their own career path.

The 1920s were one of the golden ages of collegiate life in the United States. It was the time before the Crash and between the wars, a time of raccoon coats and flappers, of the boundless optimism of youth and crisp autumn afternoons spent strolling across campuses alive with color or at the football stadium, cheering the home team to victory. Those fortunate enough to enjoy their college days in the idyllic setting of Charlottesville and the University — and their numbers had grown significantly in the past two decades, from 500 students in 1904 to 2,200 in 1929 — were doubly blessed.

Certainly Harvie always cherished his memories of life at the University. "I think that he did really find those the happiest years," agreed his wife, Letitia, many years later. "He was a natural student, and he had all the privileges and none of the responsibilities. It's about the only time in your life that you do."

During Harvie's undergraduate years (1923-27), the University's athletic teams experienced a remarkable revival under the leadership of President Edwin A. Alderman. In 1923, the varsity football team's fortunes began to improve almost immediately after former professional star Earle (Greasy) Neale was hired as its head coach. Intercollegiate boxing made its debut as a varsity sport in 1922; the University's boxing team was coached by Johnny La Rowe, a former U. S. Marine and the owner of a billiard parlor at the University since 1904. By the time Harvie graduated, boxing had become a major spectator sport, drawing 5,000 fans to bouts at the recently-built Memorial Gymnasium.

The University Band also made its inaugural appearance in the mid-1920s, and the year 1924 marked the first time that the nickname "Cavaliers" — taken from "The Cavalier Song," written by two undergraduates in 1923 — was applied to the University's teams. Since Prohibition was the law of the land, the town (which had previously housed 19 saloons on Main Street) was officially dry, though in reality only the quality of whisky consumed by the students changed, and not for the better.

In the early part of the 1920s, most of the bootleg liquor that flowed into the University came from the nearby Blue Ridge foothills. According to Virginius Dabney's study of *Mr. Jefferson's University,* emissaries from the stills would canvass the fraternity houses, calling from the front door to the residents within, "Yawl want any cawn likker today?" After a few experiences with such potent and unreliable brew, often laced with fuel oil and dead bugs, a number of undergraduates tried their hand at making their own brand of bathtub gin.

The University, of course, was still almost exclusively male, but students were free to invite female friends to visit the Grounds on weekends or on special occasions such as Easter Week, the springtime highlight of the University's social season. Formal dances — often featuring Guy Lombardo and the Royal Canadians — were held each night during Easter Week at Memorial Gym. Sometimes the festivities extended until 5 o'clock in the morning, though all social events that included women were closely chaperoned. On at least one occasion, Harvie (perhaps inadvertently, or perhaps not) invited two girlfriends for the same weekend, and enlisted the aid of a sympathetic classmate to take turns escorting the young ladies to different functions. Everything seemed to be going smoothly until Sunday evening, when it was time for the women to take the train home. Harvie had planned to have them wait at different ends of the station platform, but somehow the two chanced to meet face-to-face before the train arrived. The consequences of their encounter are not recorded in the Wilkinson archives.

As in his days at the McGuire School, Harvie proved to be an extremely diligent student, especially since he was sharing quarters with his cousin, Wilfred L. Goodwyn, Jr., at Miss Betty Cocke's famous rooming house on University Avenue, between Madison Lane and Chancellor Street. Goodwyn possessed one of the quickest minds at the University, and Harvie claimed that the experience of sharing living quarters with a roommate of such intelligence made him work three times as hard just to keep pace.

With the exception of the fateful freshman chemistry course, Harvie's academic record at the University was nearly flawless. As a result of his persistent efforts at the McGuire School, he encountered no problems even with the previously troublesome subject of mathematics; indeed, in college math again became his favorite subject, and upon Mr. McGuire's recommendation, Harvie took advanced standing in geometry and emerged as the top student in that class. Yet he also retained his love for history, language and literature, and kept Latin as one of his major fields of study. It was Harvie's firm belief, then and later, that a solid foundation in the liberal arts was the best preparation for a career in business. After he became one of the state's leading bankers, students often asked him which subjects would prepare them best for a financial career. Doubtless to their surprise, he would inform them that they would do well to major in English, because it would teach them how to write and express their ideas well. "I'll teach you banking," Harvie told them. "I'm not going to teach you how to communicate. If that doesn't appeal to you, study history, because I want someone who can learn from the past." (Accounting and economics, incidentally, finished third in Wilkinson's estimation.)

During his four years at the University, Harvie was named to Phi Beta Kappa, the Raven Society, Omicron Delta Kappa, and Alpha Kappa Psi. He joined the local chapter of Kappa Alpha fraternity, and though Harvie never pretended to be a proficient athlete, he did become an outstanding long-distance runner, and served as captain of the varsity cross-country team during his senior year. It was a sport perfectly suited for him,

Captain of the cross-country team, on the Grounds at the University of Virginia.

Harvie (front row, fifth from left) as managing editor of the University of Virginia student publication, *College Topics*.

Harvie's graduation from the University of Virginia, Phi Beta Kappa, 1927.

for it required discipline, endurance, and perseverance — qualities that Harvie Wilkinson possessed in abundance — and it called upon men to pace themselves, and keep their eyes on distant goals.

Following Harvie's graduation with an A.B. degree in 1927, his father offered him two options: he would either pay for a year of graduate study at Harvard University, or he would supplement Harvie's income in his first year of work. Eager to start his career in the financial world, Harvie chose the latter course, though it meant he would have to leave Richmond for Wall Street. "The reason I went to New York after I got out of college," he later explained, "was to obtain some knowledge of investments. There wasn't any place in Richmond then to receive such training." Accordingly, through an introduction supplied by his longtime friend Langbourne Williams, Harvie landed a job as an analyst with the investment banking firm of Lee, Higginson & Company.

The Lee Higginson Building in New York City, where
Harvie worked for nearly two years.

It was a marvelous opportunity for a young man fascinated by finance. By the
time Harvie arrived in New York late in 1927, the stock market had been rising in an
almost unbroken spiral for six years, and few observers were bold enough to predict that
the tide of rising prices might end anytime soon. Trading volume on the New York Stock
Exchange began setting records; by 1928, 920 million shares were being traded annually,
compared with only 173 million in 1921. Expert commentators claimed that the U.S.
economy had entered a New Era of perpetual prosperity, wherein poverty would be
permanently vanquished and unemployment become a thing of the past.

Public fascination with high-level financial maneuvers was fueled by rumors of
vast fortunes acquired by speculators in stocks and bonds, and so thousands of
Americans — including J. Harvie Wilkinson, Jr. — who would never have considered
placing a bet with a bookie wagered their savings on stocks of corporations such as
General Motors, U.S. Steel, and the Pennsylvania Railroad. "Taxi drivers told you what
to buy," recalled Bernard Baruch, who had already made millions of dollars in the great

bull market. "The shoe shine boy could give you a summary of the day's financial news as he worked with rag and polish. An old beggar, who regularly patrolled the street in front of my office, now gave me tips — and, I suppose, spent the money I and others gave him in the market. My cook had a brokerage account, and followed the ticker closely."

"It was a great game," joked homespun philosopher Will Rogers. "All you had to do was to buy and wait until the next morning and just pick up the paper and see how much you made, in print." Indeed, it seemed almost unpatriotic not to invest in the market. Wall Street had become a mirror of national confidence, a reflection of America's belief that the economy would keep expanding, that there were more big ideas and ambitious men waiting in the wings, that tomorrow would be even better than today.

Besides, you could buy stocks with borrowed money — in broker's terms, "on margin." Usually the down payment was no more than 10 percent, and many investors used the value of the stocks they bought as collateral for the rest of the purchase price. This process, of course, created a pyramid that depended for its stability upon continually rising prices. Once the market started to drop, investors would be forced to sell securities to meet their margin calls; and increased sales, of course, would produce further downward pressure on prices, thus sending the market into a sort of free fall.

In the halcyon bull market days of 1927-28, however, any such pessimistic scenarios seemed totally unwarranted, especially for those living in New York during the gilded reign of Mayor James J. (Gentleman Jimmy) Walker. Impeccably dressed in his trademark top hat and form-fitting, fancy clothes — including a custom-made, four-button, double-breasted black Chesterfield coat — Walker presided over New York City with a gift of laughter and a sense of high style. After spending two years in Manhattan when Walker was at the height of his charm and influence, it was no wonder that Harvie Wilkinson came to love New York as his adopted home away from home.

Harvie arrived in New York in late June 1927, and took a room at the Allerton House at 143 East 39th Street. "The Allerton House is all I expected and possibly more," he wrote to his parents in his first letter home. "My room is on the eleventh floor of a seventeen story building which is centrally located... I had been assigned a $13.50 room, but upon inquiry found that the only difference between it and a $12.50 room was size. I took the latter, which is an outside room, and though it is small answers every purpose. There is a gymnasium in the building I am glad to say."

Breakfast was available in the Allerton's dining room for 50 cents: strawberries and cream, bran muffins, tea, scrambled eggs, and bacon. (Harvie was pleased to discover that he could enjoy three good meals a day in New York for $2.00 or less.) On his first day of work — June 27 — in his chosen vocation of "practical finance," Harvie spent his time handling securities, cashing checks, delivering messages, and becoming adjusted to life "on the buzzer," in the parlance of stock market clerks. Within a few months, he had moved up to enjoy more responsibility in Lee, Higginson's statistical and correspondence department.

Even though Harvie's options, in terms of an evening's entertainment, were somewhat restricted by his income, his instinct toward thrift, and the demands of his job, he developed a lasting fondness for certain landmark New York institutions, including the tea room at the Plaza, Giovanni's Restaurant, and especially the St. Regis Hotel and its King Cole Bar, to which Harvie always paid a sentimental visit whenever he returned to New York in later years. One could obtain a fascinating education simply by watching the comings and goings of personalities at such well-known locations in the late 1920s; it was at the St. Regis, for instance, that Harvie often observed the surrealist and wholly unconventional artist Salvador Dali in the King Cole Bar, sitting alone, sipping a martini.

Harvie also did his best to keep up with current events, though on the limited budget that remained after paying for the necessities and making his investments, he decided he could afford to purchase only one five-cent newspaper a day. So he bought a copy of the *New York Times* in the morning, and saved half of it to read in the afternoon. Once Harvie sent his parents a detailed copy of his budget, down to the single nickel he spent on his daily paper, and his father replied with alacrity. "Son, here's an increase in your allowance," wrote Mr. Wilkinson. "But don't ever do that to your mother again. When you said you could only afford one newspaper a day, she was nearly in tears for fear that you were in a dire position."

Although he enjoyed life in Manhattan, Harvie clearly missed his home in Richmond and the opportunity to discuss daily matters with his parents, and particularly with his father. "At times," he wrote to his parents, "I get very discouraged but try to keep on. And thus you see you have an extremely vital place in my life. Continue to give me your counsel, and I value it highly. You know full well I heed your advice even though I make gyrations."

And shortly before he left Lee, Higginson in February 1929, Harvie noted in a letter to his mother that "if I had some of [Dad's] virtues and characteristics, especially a great fund of knowledge acquired through many years of experience, I should consider myself most fortunate. I have come into contact with supposedly smart men and I venture to say that in any line Dad had gone in he would have made a success. His judgment is always worth listening to, and there will be quite a feeling of safety when I return home and have his viewpoint on tap, even though I am leaving this field of so-called savants."

In the early winter of 1929, Harvie decided that it was time to return to his native Virginia, and so he left Lee, Higginson — though he retained many of the contacts he had made with members of the financial community on Wall Street — and accepted a position as a security analyst and statistician in the recently-formed investment department of the State-Planters Bank and Trust Company in Richmond. Eight months later, the stock market suffered the worst disaster in its history, as security prices across the board plummeted in the Great Crash. □

II

PORTRAIT OF A BANKER

Total man is the central theme of
Virginians, perhaps more so than in most
of the states. In part this stems from
closeness to the soil, in part from the
heavy influence of the church…
Southerners value the personal equation,
and their assessment of it, for they have
long lived close to nature's realm.

— J. HARVIE WILKINSON, JR.

Even before the events of Black Tuesday (October 29, 1929) on Wall Street, Harvie Wilkinson had lost the paper fortune he had accumulated — in his case, about $3,000 — in one of the stock market's violent and terrifying downturns, and he suddenly found himself in debt to the equivalent of nearly a year's salary. And yet Wilkinson considered himself lucky, because he still had his job at State-Planters, and he knew he would be able to pay off his debts. "He often said it was the greatest lesson he ever learned," recalled Lewis Wilkinson, Harvie's younger son. In later years, Harvie frequently counseled his subordinates "not to try to make money quickly," because "money quickly and easily made is money quickly and easily spent." Or lost in speculative ventures.

When Wilkinson joined State-Planters Bank and Trust in 1929, it was not the largest bank in Richmond — that honor belonged to its main competitor, the First and Merchants Bank — but it did rank as the foremost source of corporate loans and investments. Actually, State-Planters had been formed only three years earlier, by a merger of two of the city's most historic and prestigious financial institutions, the State & City Bank and Trust Company, and the Planters National Bank.

Planters National was the heir of the Farmers Bank, which originally had been chartered in Richmond in February 1812 as only the second Virginia bank with statewide connections. Located in its early years in a corner house below the Eagle Tavern, on the south side of Main between Twelfth and Thirteenth Streets, the Farmers Bank was a pioneer in the financing of the early railroad system in the United States. Not surprisingly, considering its place of prominence in the capital of the Confederacy, the bank also played a substantial role in financing the South's government during the war years between 1861 and 1865. When General Lee's surrender at Appomattox in the spring of 1865 rendered all Confederate securities useless, the Farmers Bank was forced into failure along with every other bank in Richmond.

Later that same year, however, a new institution, known as the Planters National Bank, rose from the ashes of Farmers. In December 1865, the new bank received a national charter, and subsequently established its headquarters at Twelfth and Main Streets. In its early years, Planters was led by many of the chief officers of its illustrious and late predecessor, including the renowned Richmond lawyer and financier William H. Macfarland, whose tireless dedication to civic and philanthropic affairs would provide a model for Harvie Wilkinson nearly a century later. By 1870, as the region began at last to recover from the war, the growing need for capital convinced Macfarland and several colleagues that Richmond required yet another bank. The result was the State Bank of Virginia, whose operations at the outset were directed by Macfarland from modest beginnings in a corner of a general store at the corner of Eleventh and Main. Within three years, the bank had expanded its operations sufficiently to require larger quarters at 1111 Main Street.

As one might expect, relations between State and Planters remained close throughout the late 19th century. Planters continued to focus its attention upon financing the city's burgeoning variety of industrial enterprises, including manufacturers of iron, paper, drugs, flour, locomotives, and building materials, as well as providing capital for home construction, transportation systems, and the state's traditional tobacco trade. State Bank, meanwhile, obtained a national charter in 1907 and changed its name to

Top: Planters National Bank, at 12th and Main Streets, about 1921.

Above: National State & City Bank at 1111 East Main Street in 1921 with the Federal Reserve Bank of Richmond, to the right, at 1109 East Main Street.

State-Planters Bank and Trust Company at the corner of Ninth and Main Streets in 1925, with the Rueger Hotel and Capitol Bell Tower in the background.

The State-Planters Bank Lobby during the grand opening of the building in 1924.

Julien H. Hill, President, National State & City Bank;
President, State & City Bank and Trust Co.; President,
State-Planters Bank and Trust Company.

National State Bank. Over the following two decades, it embarked upon a series of
mergers with other banks in the area — most notably the City Bank of Richmond
(1910), the Old Dominion Trust Company (1922), and the Broad Street Bank (1925) —
at the conclusion of which it emerged as the State & City Bank and Trust Company.

   The union of the Planters with State & City in 1926, therefore, had created a
financial organization of imposing strength and stature. The first president of the State-
Planters was Julien Harrison Hill, whose father, William M. Hill, had been first
vice-president of National State & City Bank. Julien Hill had started his career at the
bank as a runner, working his way up through the ranks — as was the custom in the
banking community in those days — and learning the business as a cashier and vice
president before assuming the top leadership role.

   One of the challenges facing Hill and his colleagues at State-Planters in the late
1920s involved the employment of the bank's capital in bond investments. For most
banks in the United States, bond accounts — and, indeed, securities investments in

The Sun of Prosperity

gilds the horizon of 1930. The anxieties of recent
months are behind us. The courage, resourcefulness
and vision characteristic of our people assure the
return of prosperity normal for a country with vast
resources and earning power intact.

During the coming year, as in the past, our resources, financial knowledge, and experience (gained
during sixty-four years of successful banking) will
be used to further the industrial and commercial interests of the territory we serve.

We invite opportunities for co-operation.

STATE-PLANTERS
BANK AND TRUST CO.
RICHMOND   VIRGINIA

Commercial — Savings — Trust — Investment — Mortgage — Safe Deposit Vaults

This message of hope and encouragement to the Richmond
business community appeared in the *Richmond Times-Dispatch*
during the dark days after the crash, January 1930.

general — were then a relatively novel tool, and one whose functions were as yet only dimly understood by many bankers. With the notable exception of the nation's most powerful financial institutions, American banks traditionally had used their capital primarily for loans, either to commercial enterprises or creditworthy individuals. But the nation's entry into World War I had created a veritable explosion of credit, awakening banks to the virtues of investment in government bonds, and the subsequent period of economic expansion during the following decade had made industrial bonds appear equally attractive. Small banks in the South and Midwest, and large banks in the eastern cities began purchasing bonds, and urged their depositors to go and do likewise.

Since the prices of virtually every type of security continued to rise throughout most of the 1920s, banks did not always scrutinize prospective bond offerings with great care before making an investment. The short-sightedness of such a policy was brought home with painful force once the Crash occurred and bond prices began to tumble. Moreover, the ensuing Depression quickly froze the demand for commercial loans, as it dulled banks' willingness to make such loans. Yet if the banks' traditional capital outlet of business loans were closed, they would need to find some other alternative, and the bond market appeared to offer one of the few viable alternatives.

And this was precisely where Harvie Wilkinson entered the picture. Before Wilkinson arrived, State-Planters had not employed a professional, trained securities analyst. In fact, for several years, Harvie — together with a few clerks and secretaries — essentially was the bank's investment department. It was State-Planters' good fortune to have Wilkinson at the bank during this critical period of radical change in investment strategy during the early 1930s, because other banks without similarly qualified and experienced investment officers suffered appalling losses from imprudent bond selections. Indeed, a majority of the bank failures during the deflationary period of 1930-33 were attributed to the poor performance of those institutions' bond portfolios. (Fortunately, Richmond's economy was sufficiently diversified to spare the city the worst ravages of the Depression, as only one of the major Richmond banks actually failed during the immediate crisis.)

Under Harvie Wilkinson's leadership, the State-Planters investment department, which handled investments for both the bank itself and its trust department, prospered and expanded. In June 1931, the bank named Wilkinson manager of the investment department. Two years later, he was appointed an assistant vice president at a salary of $250 a month, and in January 1935 Harvie became a full vice president — the youngest at State-Planters. By that time, James W. Rawles, a fellow graduate of the University of Virginia (as well as the Harvard Business School) and the brother of one of Harvie's closest friends, Dr. Benjamin Rawles, had joined the bank's investment department to help Wilkinson deal with the growing volume of business. According to Rawles, Julien Hill allowed Harvie virtually a free hand in making investment decisions for the bank and, to a slightly lesser extent, for the State-Planters Trust Department as well.

While he was managing the investment affairs of State-Planters, Wilkinson also found time to teach classes in finance at several of the local colleges. In 1929-30, he served as adjunct professor at the University of Virginia, and for much of the following decade he taught evening courses in finance at the University of Richmond, and at Virginia Mechanics Institute, where educational courses from the American Bankers Association were taught. Meanwhile, Harvie continued his own education at the Graduate School of Banking at Rutgers University, also sponsored by the ABA, and was a member of that school's first graduating class in 1937.

For his graduate thesis, Wilkinson wrote a comprehensive study on responsible bond investment strategies for banks. Subsequently published in 1938 by Harper & Brothers under the title of *Investment Policies for Commercial Banks*, Wilkinson's book was a highly-praised, landmark volume that outlined the fundamentals of sound investment procedures for bankers who were under considerable stress to expand their investments without risking extensive losses.

One of Wilkinson's main purposes in writing *Investment Policies* was to correct certain misapprehensions within the banking community about bonds and their proper use. First, he argued that bonds had been (and still were) "erroneously regarded as a liquid rather than as a shiftable asset." Not surprisingly, bankers had therefore treated bonds as their first line of defense against a run on reserves, but they had been rudely disillusioned when their security accounts failed to perform adequately in that capacity. Unlike commercial loans, which were not looked upon as a line of defense at all, bankers were endeavoring to have their bond accounts "fulfill a function which by their very nature they cannot!"

Wilkinson then proceeded to lay out a strategy whereby banks could employ their investments in a more prudent and profitable fashion. The key, according to Wilkinson, was to make a clear distinction between a secondary reserve — that is, "the first line of defense which will be employed to replenish the primary reserve whenever that reserve needs to be replenished because of withdrawals of deposits or an increase in loan demand — and a bond investment account." For the former, Wilkinson recommended that banks use only prime securities with short maturities, preferably four years or less, with maturities staggered over the four-year cycle.

Only after an adequate secondary reserve had been established should a bank seek to purchase securities for its bond investment account. The function of that account, as Wilkinson viewed it, was "to earn the bank an interest return on a portion of its funds which cannot be safely and properly loaned out in the community and which are not required for the secondary reserve account." Like most bankers of his era, Wilkinson believed that banks were in business to lend money in the communities and areas in which they served; that they had, in fact, an obligation to make those loans prior to placing any funds in an investment account. Rather than risk marginal loans, however, Wilkinson clearly advocated the purchase of bonds: "An adequately selected bond investment is far preferable to a marginal or even a second grade loan."

Depending upon the quality of the bonds selected, and of course the experience and expertise of the bank's investment personnel, Wilkinson recommended that banks limit their bond investment portfolio to an amount between two and one-half and four times the net capital funds allocated to the support of bonds. Under no circumstances, insisted Wilkinson, should the greater limit be exceeded, else banks would risk total disaster if bond prices were to suffer declines similar to those witnessed in 1929-33.

Wilkinson's conclusions reflected well the essential conservatism of his emerging banking philosophy, and his faith in the ability of informed, forward-looking financiers to make better judgments about banking issues than legislators or bureaucrats. "American banking must prepare itself," he maintained,

> to diagnose the credit risk in bonds as it has in the past diagnosed the credit risk in loans. More and more does this seem inevitable as industry finances itself through our capital markets.

Harvie with Lewis F. Powell, Jr. on Powell's wedding
day in 1936.

Legislation cannot be the final answer to the bond problem confronting
banks. No dicta can be laid down which will fully protect the banking
system. This division of our national economy must demonstrate that it is
possessed of sufficient flexibility to meet the needs of a dynamic society.
There can be no lasting solution which is childlike in its simplicity.

Not long after his return to Richmond, Harvie had resumed his friendship with
Lewis Powell, who had joined the law firm of Hunton & Williams shortly after his
graduation from Harvard Law School. The two men had seen very little of each other
since their days at the McGuire School, but they quickly picked up their relationship
with hardly a missed beat. Their favorite rendezvous for lunch was the Occidental
Restaurant, where they could obtain an excellent meal for only fifty cents (a not insig-
nificant consideration for two young professionals during the depths of the Depression,

especially since Powell's wife, Jo, had put him on an allowance of one dollar per day), while they discussed their plans for the future.

"Our short-term objectives were merely to survive economically," recalled Powell, "but we were dreamers, and we decided that we'd like to be important people in Richmond and the state, and we thought about ways that would move us in that direction." Later, of course, they would be joined by Virginius Dabney and George Gibson, and the conversation would veer from serious discussions of current political and economic topics, to less weighty matters ranging from professional baseball, ballet, and sixteenth-century French furniture to the intriguing contents of D. H. Lawrence's controversial novel, *Lady Chatterley's Lover*. (The other three members of the group teased V. Dabney mercilessly when the journalist admitted that he had never read the book.)

During the 1930s, Wilkinson and Powell also enjoyed the company of another, larger circle of friends known as the Lonely Hearts Club. Originally, the "Lonelies," as they called themselves, consisted of about a dozen Richmond-area men in their late twenties and early thirties, who — being possessed of substantial intellectual curiosity but rather little cash — agreed to meet once a month to discuss various subjects of mutual interest. At nearly the same time, a number of similarly-minded young women, all of whom were college graduates (including Frances Leigh Williams, who later became one of Virginia's leading writers), formed their own distaff version of the Lonelies. Not surprisingly, the two groups — both men and women — soon decided that it would be even more interesting to hold their meetings together.

Looking back from the perspective of the 1990s, there is something touching, sweet, and refreshingly honest about this youthful fraternity. Their gatherings seem to have been entirely platonic, as witnessed by the fact that none of them married within the group. Certainly it was an elitist company, in the sense that the Lonelies all considered themselves among the city's leading intellectual lights. "The truth is," observed Powell, "that Harvie had a weakness for members of the opposite sex whose intellectual attainments he admired. Some of his chauvinist friends thought that this limited the field somewhat, but Harvie persisted in his high standards." Typically their meetings began with a presentation or lecture by one or more members — Harvie would talk about investments, perhaps, or Lewis Powell would recount a recent conversation with Justice

Lonely Hearts Club (back row, left to right) O.T. Jamerson, Fielding Williams, Turner Arrington, Samuel Jackson, Mary Anderson (Mrs. Deane Ribble); (front row, left to right) Betty Taylor (Mrs. Edgar Rust), Peggy Patterson (Mrs. Patterson Ruddock), Harvie Wilkinson, Betty Patterson (Mrs. John Page Williams), Nora Lee Antrim. Not pictured are Mate Branch (Mrs. Henry Converse), Jack Davis, Lewis Powell, Frances Leigh Williams.

Felix Frankfurter of the U.S. Supreme Court — followed by a discussion, and then a pick-up dinner.

As time went on, though, the Lonelies' gatherings grew more social and less concerned with highbrow affairs. One of the highlights of the group's life was an extended weekend trip to New York City. "That was a great event," remembered Powell years later, "though I think the parents thought this was a bad idea," since members of both sexes would be traveling on the same overnight train to Manhattan. As the only Lonely who had spent much time in New York, Harvie arranged for rooms for everyone at his favorite hotel, the St. Regis. He then reserved several tables for dinner at the Plaza, where Eddy Duchin's Orchestra was appearing nightly. Before the evening was over, the rest of the restaurant's patrons had been treated to the sight of the normally sedate Frances Williams dancing on top of one of the tables.

When the group returned to the St. Regis — where they had all taken rooms on the same floor — Harvie playfully decided to pay a call on the young ladies. "He said he was going to visit the girls," recalled Lewis Powell, "but the house detective was tipped off by somebody — it may have been somebody in our group — and he caught Harvie. So we had to identify him as a member of our group, and the girls all certified that he had behaved himself. By accident, of course," said Powell with a chuckle, "I happened to be nearby, and was barely able to forestall a formal charge."

In April 1935, Harvie celebrated his twenty-ninth birthday, still a bachelor and a member of the Lonely Hearts. But he would not retain his unmarried status for long. That summer, Harvie and Lewis Powell decided to take their vacation at Woodberry Forest, a private boys' school in the country north of Richmond which doubled as an inn in the summertime. Harvie's father was in ailing health at the time — and would, in fact, die less than a year later — and so Harvie was reluctant to be away from central Virginia for any extended period. Hence he chose Woodberry, where his parents were staying, for a brief retreat, and Powell agreed to accompany him.

On Saturday nights, the Woodberry School frequently sponsored dances for their summer school students and youth from the surrounding area. Reluctantly, because most of the guests were younger than they, Harvie and Lewis decided to attend one of the parties. After they arrived, Lewis spotted a young lady named Letitia Strother Nelson, one of his sister's friends from Hollins College who had stayed at the Powell home during school breaks. Lewis brought Harvie over and introduced him to Letitia, and there were absolutely no sparks at all between the couple. "I thought, 'He's a very nice fellow, but he's considerably older, and I'm not interested,'" Letitia later confided. "I thought he was staid and sedate; he thought I was frivolous."

Perhaps. But after she graduated from Hollins in 1936 and took several courses at a business school in Wilmington, Delaware, Letitia went to Richmond in the summer of 1937 to look for a job. Among other places, she applied for a position at State-Planters, where there was an opening for a secretary in the investment department. As the head of the department and a member of the bank's personnel committee, Harvie naturally interviewed Letitia for the job, and he was quite taken with her. He later recalled the incident with great clarity and affection.

She had on a large Scotch plaid, and a big Panama hat, and I was simply struck dumb. I said to myself, "If I can marry the girl, I will do so." But I also said, "I've got to find exactly what her status is."

Accordingly, I said, "Miss Nelson, one of our problems here is that we get young girls like you in here, they are engaged, and in a year they are gone. Are you engaged?"

"No," she said, "I am not."

I said, "The next problem is that they may not technically be engaged, and hence your answer is quite truthful, but you also may have a steady beau, with whom you may become engaged tonight."

She said, "I have no such person."

And then I said to myself, "I think I'll enter the race."

Before the interview ended, Harvie asked Letitia what she enjoyed doing in her spare time. She replied that she loved to read the *Wall Street Journal* and the financial section of the *New York Times*. Now, Harvie realized that there likely was a touch of falsehood in Miss Nelson's answer, but he decided that if she had enough bluff to give that sort of reply, she probably would get along fine in the department. And so Harvie offered her the job as the second secretary, and Letitia accepted, despite warnings from other secretaries during a coffee break that Harvie was "the fastest dictator and used the biggest words" of any executive at the bank. She remained in the investment department, however, for only six months, and for at least two of those months Harvie was in Europe on a business trip for the bank. When an opening appeared in the bank's advertising and public relations department, Letitia took the job, and found it far more satisfying to write copy rather than take dictation or type.

Shortly after Harvie's return, he asked Letitia for a date, and the romance had begun. The circumstances of their first date are, perhaps, worth recounting. "He told me he was going to take me to a movie," remembered Letitia, "but he took me driving. And I said to myself, 'Uh-oh, we're going to have to be very careful.' Then, when he drove us over what was then Huguenot Bridge, which was a very little one-way bridge, he stopped the car and reached for my hand. I said, 'None of this. This is entirely unwholesome, Mr. Wilkinson.' 'Unwholesome' was an expression we used to use at Hollins when people

Letitia Strother Nelson on her wedding day, October 14, 1939.

The honeymooners at Sea Island, Georgia, looking very pleased with themselves.

made a pass at us. That usually made them laugh, and it worked. Well, Harvie didn't laugh very much, but he did continue to get over the bridge, and we finally got to the movie. But that was not his intention."

Knowing how thoroughly dedicated Harvie was to his work at the bank, and how much in love he was with Letitia, Harvie's friends went to considerable lengths to make certain that he took enough time from work for courting, for he was still a very sober and industrious young man. Unlike later years, when he assembled a wardrobe renowned for its variety and style, Harvie wore only dark gray, almost black suits which he invariably wore with white shirts and a stiff white, detached collar. "It was Harvie's conviction," recalled one of his friends with a chuckle, "that to succeed in those drab, depression days one must look as drab as the times. But the suit really did give him a very distinguished appearance."

As it turned out, Harvie's friends need not have worried. By the summer of 1939, Mr. Wilkinson and Miss Nelson were engaged. They were married on October 14, 1939, in St. Stephen's Episcopal Church in Culpeper, Virginia, where the Nelsons had been members for several generations. (Wilfred Goodwyn, Harvie's cousin and former roommate, who by then was head of his own investment firm in Washington, D.C., served as best man.) Harvie had planned to take his bride to Europe for their honeymoon, but war had just broken out on that continent; and though there was little military action at the time, the situation was so unsettled that State-Planters president Julien Hill asked Harvie to delay his journey. Instead, the Wilkinsons spent their honeymoon at The Cloisters in Sea Island, Georgia.

During the next two years, the U.S. economy underwent rapid growth, stimulated by President Franklin Delano Roosevelt's preparedness program, with its vast increases in defense spending. Certainly State-Planters was as pleased to witness the recovery as any financial institution in the central Virginia area, for its credit accounts — and especially the mortgage loans it had made in significant numbers for the first time in the easy money days of the late 1920s — had been suffering severely during the mid-1930s. In the single year of 1935, for instance, the bank had been forced to charge off 5 percent of its loan portfolio.

Indeed, the entire period from 1932 to 1941 could be considered a period of eclipse for State-Planters and, in fact, the entire banking profession in the United States. The stigma attached to banks during the Depression took the prestige and popularity of banking to one of the lowest points in American history. For State-Planters in particular, it was a period of fighting for survival, of conservation, and rebuilding the financial strength of the bank in anticipation of future expansion.

By the end of this troubled decade, State-Planters had regained its health, but it remained a relatively small institution by modern standards, with slightly less than $50 million in assets, and approximately 150 employees, including 50 officers, with quarters in two-and-one-half floors of the bank's 13-story headquarters building on Ninth and Main Streets in downtown Richmond. The investment department, meanwhile, had grown to include three executives: Harvie Wilkinson, Jim Rawles, and Moncure P. Patteson. Beyond his duties at the bank, Harvie also found time in 1940 to lecture on investments at Rutgers University as a member of the faculty of the Graduate School of Banking of the American Bankers Association.

Top: Harvie lecturing at the Graduate School of Banking, Rutgers University, June 1940.

Above: The banking lobby of State-Planters Bank in 1940 showing decorations and cake to celebrate its 75th anniversary.

Senior officers of State-Planters Bank in 1940 with a combined total of 268 years of banking experience. From left to right: Messrs. Richard H. Smith, Chairman Executive Committee; Wilson M. Brown, Vice President; Warren M. Goddard, Vice President; J. Harvie Wilkinson, Jr., Vice President; Julien H. Hill, President; Jesse F. Wood, Vice President; Harry H. Augustine, Vice President, and E. E. Wilson, Vice President.

Junior officers of State-Planters Bank in 1940. From left to right: Messrs. L. W. Bishop, Cashier; J. W. Rawles, Assistant Cashier; E. F. Gee, Assistant Cashier; R. H. Wells, Assistant Cashier; M. P. Patteson, Assistant Cashier; C. R. Davis, Assistant Vice President; O. T. Jamerson, Assistant Trust Officer; T. R. Salley, Manager Real Estate Department; J. C. Davis, Assistant Cashier, and L. B. Gunn, Trust Officer.

As the pace of the nation's defense buildup continued to increase in the winter of 1940-41, Harvie urged his colleagues in the Virginia business community to do whatever they could to assist the government's efforts. "We must bestir ourselves immediately," he told the annual meeting of the Virginia Bankers Association on January 25, 1941, "and be alert and aggressive in coping successfully with this gigantic program."

> We have yet no dream of what this armament program will amount to, but it is going to be with us for years to come. We are going to have to bring to bear all the experience we have had in dealing with our customers…

> American business and the banking fraternity are not lacking in patriotism. Businessmen are going to do business with the Government, and the sooner we step out, and not shy off, the better off we will be.

Early in 1941, Julien Hill retired and Harry Hamill Augustine assumed the presidency of State-Planters. A tall, blonde man with steel-blue eyes, Augustine looked every inch the part of a bank president. He had acquired a well-deserved reputation as an

Harry Hamill Augustine, President, State-Planters Bank, 1941-1958.

45

Lobby of State-Planters shortly after the outbreak of World War II. As employees joined the armed services, their names were placed on a board behind the teller line and a star for each was added to the board above the listings.

By the end of the war, the list of State-Planters' employees in the armed services had grown appreciably.

extremely conservative banker — which should not have surprised anyone, considering the parlous condition of the banking industry in the 1930s — but also proved to be an adept administrator who particularly valued order and leadership. Wilkinson, who admired Augustine deeply, later described him as a man of unusually sound judgment, great common sense, and "one of the best judges of character I ever saw."

Almost as soon as Augustine took office, however, the nation was plunged into World War II. Harvie Wilkinson, for one, had no illusions about the struggle that lay ahead, for those on the home front as well as the troops on the front line. "Winter winds will sweep the shelves," he predicted in a speech before the Richmond Community Council on January 14, 1942. "We will pay terrific taxes and work longer hours. We will hoard grease drippings. We will wash without benefit of lather."

About a month later, Harvie (who was then thirty-five years old) joined the Special Financial Services Division of the U. S. Army. Starting as a captain in the Advance Payment and Loan Branch, he was initially stationed at the Pentagon, where he and his colleagues had the responsibility of assessing the financial soundness of companies that were awarded prime defense contracts, and then supervising government guaranteed loans to those firms.

Lieutenant Colonel J. Harvie Wilkinson, Jr. 1945.

Harvie with his son Jay in spring, 1945,
in New York City.

After a year and a half, Wilkinson was transferred to New York to perform similar duties for the Special Services Division at the New York Federal Reserve Bank. By all accounts, Harvie — by then Lieutenant Colonel Wilkinson — seems to have found his wartime duties reasonably rewarding, and certainly his investment training made him quite adept at carrying out the sort of in-depth analysis his assignment required. He and Letitia lived at 7 Gracie Square, just across from Carl Schurz Park and not far from the Mayor's Mansion; in fact, while walking to and from his home, Harvie occasionally saw Mayor Fiorello LaGuardia, the legendary "Little Flower," who would greet him with a hearty, "Hi, soldier!"

While they were still in New York, the Wilkinsons' first child — James Harvie Wilkinson III — was born on September 29, 1944. Less than a year later, the war ended with the surrender of the imperial Japanese government, and the process of demobilization began. As the time for his discharge neared, several prestigious Manhattan banks approached Harvie to ascertain his interest in coming to work for them, but he firmly discouraged all such inquiries. He decided instead to return to Virginia, to Richmond, and the State-Planters Bank.

Richmond in the autumn of 1946 seemed to have changed very little since the war began; no more had State-Planters. The demands of the war effort had boosted the city's industrial capacity, and many manufacturing plants had been temporarily converted to defense-oriented production, but the primary changes wrought by the war were less visible, and would take considerable time to make themselves apparent to all. In terms of politics, finance, and race relations, Richmond — and Virginia — was being thrust into the mid-twentieth century (whether willingly or not), and it required men and women of vision and courage to recognize that fact and act upon its implications.

It was clear to professional businessmen such as Harvie Wilkinson that the Virginia financial community would need to undergo broad and substantial changes in the postwar world, and it was this imperative that helped convince Wilkinson to return to his native state in 1946. A challenge awaited him there, an exciting opportunity to make a crucial, lasting contribution to the economic welfare of Virginia by adapting the best of the South's traditions to the new era. "He knew what his mission was in Virginia," noted Harvie's elder son, Jay. "He knew what he wanted to do in Virginia — to take the rather fragmented banking world and build some larger aggregations of capital within the state which would serve as a source of capital for businesses coming into the state, and help Virginia take off into the modern commercial age."

Upon his return to Richmond in April 1946, Harvie Wilkinson was elected to the board of directors of State-Planters Bank and Trust Company. He remained one of the bank's vice presidents, of course, and head of the investment department. Far more than most of his colleagues on the board or in the executive offices at State-Planters, Harvie Wilkinson realized that banking could no longer remain in the same comfortable mold that had sufficed before the war. Certainly Harvie was inherently more aggressive, more willing to investigate new avenues and experiment with innovations than the vast majority of Virginia bankers in the late 1940s. Perhaps the fact that his experience had centered around the field of investment banking, rather than commercial lending — the traditional training ground of bank executives — had enhanced his willingness to take risks.

In any event, Harvie saw that banks would need to acquire officers with greater expertise in specialized areas if they were to prosper in the postwar era, and that meant that they would have to open their doors to prospective officers from a far broader range of socio-economic backgrounds than they traditionally had done. As a member of the State-Planters personnel committee, Wilkinson also realized that the bank needed to substantially alter its traditional salary and benefit policies to meet the challenges of the postwar period. In a formal report to Harry Augustine in mid-1946, Harvie and his colleagues on the committee urged the bank to increase its salary levels (particularly for longtime employees) to keep pace with wages in industry, to enhance employee morale by introducing scientific management policies and improved fringe benefits (including the establishment of a "State-Planters Club" whose avowed purpose was "to promote social intercourse among the employees"), to initiate recruitment efforts at colleges and universities throughout the region, and to recognize, in short, that the bank could no longer afford a traditional paternalistic attitude that assumed employee loyalty without active encouragement on the part of management.

Both Wilkinson and his longtime friend, Lewis F. Powell, Jr., recognized a similar need for modernization in the political sphere. In fact, by the time that Powell — who had been working on the highly classified "Ultra" code-breaking project during the war — returned to Richmond in 1946, he found the city in considerable ferment over the drive to reform the outmoded and extraordinarily inefficient structure of municipal government. "It's hard to believe," Powell observed years later, "that any city had the type of government that we had at that time."

Basically, Richmond's government consisted of a mayor, a board of aldermen, and a board of common council, and any legislation submitted had to be passed at all three levels. Almost invariably, the result was near-complete deadlock and stagnation. During the war, a band of forward-looking citizens had organized the Richmond Citizens Association to spearhead a drive to adopt a less unwieldy government structure. Shortly after his return, Harvie gave much of his time and influence to the movement, as did Powell. When the public finally had a chance to vote on the membership of a charter reform commission, the ticket recommended by the Citizens Association won in a popular landslide. With Powell as its chairman, the commission drew up a plan for a nine-member Council, elected at large on a nonpartisan basis, and a city manager chosen by the Council.

In a special referendum in November 1947, the voters of Richmond overwhelmingly endorsed the new charter. It was a measure of the stature that Harvie Wilkinson had already attained within the community that he — along with Powell — was asked to serve as one of the initial members of the Council. Both men, however, regretfully declined the honor, due to their already extensive professional and civic commitments.

Wilkinson's efforts on behalf of charter reform represented only a small fraction of the time he spent on behalf of educational, religious, and charitable organizations in the immediate postwar period. Before he married Letitia, Harvie had consented to join the Episcopal Church; previously, he had been a member of Richmond's Seventh Street Christian Church, where he had served as deacon and Sunday School superintendent. They decided to join St. James's Episcopal Church in the city, and Harvie soon began offering his time — as well as his financial means — to the service of the church in a variety of areas.

St. James's was one of the most historic churches in Richmond, tracing its lineage back to 1835. When it moved into its present building on West Franklin Street in 1913, it was still on the western edge of the city, surrounded by vast tracts of rural land. For generations, its work was guided by those whom Harvie referred to as "wonderful historical families who saw to it that, as churches of that time should be, St. James's was comfortable both by virtue of a good plant and pleasant pastoral sermons designed to give comfort as between the coming choices of heaven and hell." Beginning with the end of World War II, however, the pace of change quickened, and the nature of the congregation of St. James's and the location of its members inevitably changed and evolved as the residential development of the city spread westward.

Not surprisingly, much of Harvie Wilkinson's work for the church came in the areas of financial affairs and executive leadership. In 1940 he had served as chairman of the church's every member canvass. Upon his return from the war, Harvie — in addition to serving on the Vestry — was elected and re-elected to a number of church committees ranging from a special committee on rates and salaries to the church's investment committee, even serving as a subcommittee of one to employ his extensive expertise in bonds.

Perhaps his most cherished service, however, came in the areas of education and stewardship. For forty years, Harvie served as a member of the Board of Trustees of the Church Schools in the Diocese of Virginia, which for him was a true labor of love. This corporation had been founded in 1920 by the Episcopal Church in the Diocese as part of

St. James's Episcopal Church, Richmond, as it looked in 1926.

an effort to spread the values of Christianity and democracy. By the time Harvie joined the board in 1948, there were seven schools in the system, including St. Christopher's School and St. Catherine's School in Richmond, with a total enrollment of approximately 3,000 students.

All seven schools operated on the premise that Christian education was as important as any other academic subject, and each was grounded in the philosophical view that mankind alone was not the measure of the world. Along with the usual college preparatory subjects, they offered courses in ethics, the history of the Church, and the history of the Old and New Testaments. In short, they combined idealism with a healthy sense of realism, in an effort to prepare their students intellectually, physically, morally, and spiritually for the rest of their lives. It was a combination that naturally appealed to Harvie Wilkinson, who brought to the Board his expertise in both finance and education. When the Church Schools formed a search committee to look for their first full-time dean, they naturally turned to Harvie to serve as a member of the committee.

Whenever the Church Schools were in the midst of one of their special steward-ship campaigns, Harvie could be counted on to deliver an extremely persuasive message on the obligations of Christian stewardship. As one high-ranking church official with an affinity for the Book of Genesis put it, "Only Harvie could peer into the abyss; when the constituency and coffers of Church Schools seemed without form and void, and the spirit of the skeptics moved upon the face of the Schools; [Harvie would] speak into the deep pockets, saying, 'Let there be gifts,' and there were gifts. 'Be fruitful and multiply,' he said, 'and have dominion over the Old Dominion.' And behold the endowment of Church Schools and of the individual Schools increased manyfold." "Had Harvie's hopes been less bold and his strength of lesser proportions," noted former Dean Christopher M. Brookfield, "the endowment initiative would never have gotten off the ground."

But stewardship for Harvie Wilkinson meant more than an occasional message on giving or an annual campaign for funds. To him, it represented a deeply felt need to repay the community, and God, for the blessings he had received in his life. At no time did Harvie feel this obligation more clearly than when he returned to Richmond at the end of the war. In his later years, Wilkinson noted that "when I was about forty years old, I thought it very essential to set the value scale of my life. I did not see how it was possible for one person to be more fortunate than I was: born in the United States, in the Commonwealth of Virginia, in the city of Richmond, of two simply magnificent parents." At that moment, he resolved with renewed determination to attempt to repay this debt as far as he was physically and financially able through his life and actions. "Foremost in my mind," he declared, "was to try to discharge my obligations. I accordingly came to determine not to accumulate money beyond what I was hoping and praying was going to be sufficient for my family. The rest, if good fortune gave me any, I determined to give away, as one form of liquidating my debt to society, for all society had given me."

Beyond his work for the church, Wilkinson also contributed his time and talents to numerous charitable organizations in the Richmond area, including among others the Richmond Memorial Hospital, the Hollywood Memorial Association, and the Retreat for the Sick Hospital. During the Depression, he had served for several years as chairman of the speakers' bureau of the local Community Fund campaign, organizing corps of speakers to put across the message of the charity to a wide variety of audiences. Harvie resumed his activity in the postwar years, accepting a nomination to the board of trustees of the

Richmond Area Community Chest (now the United Way of Greater Richmond and Southside Virginia). In 1952, as general of the Community Chest fund drive, he led that organization to its first successful campaign in several years. Four years later, he was elected president of the Community Chest, and carried out a reorganization of the charity's executive, budget, finance, and headquarters committees.

Renowned as a public speaker — both for his command of the English language and his sparkling wit — Harvie seldom turned down an opportunity to talk to any captive audience about financial matters. He seemed especially eager to inform women's organizations (such as the Virginia Federation of Women's Clubs, and the Junior League) about the finer points of investing. Upon such occasions, he usually stuck to the basics of investment strategy, providing his listeners (most of whom were, after all, novices in the financial world) with such sound and easily remembered advice as, "When you buy stocks can be almost as important as what you buy"; "Buy at the right time and buy the right stock"; and "Too much intuition and not enough mathematics won't mix in the stock market." "Investing is an art with a scientific base," he insisted. "It is not solely an art, not only a science."

Occasionally, Harvie would journey west to Charlottesville, to speak before undergraduate audiences at the University. In the late autumn of 1946, for instance, he delivered the inaugural speech in a series of lectures by prominent businessmen on the subject of vocational guidance. It was an especially timely topic, in view of the numerous veterans and older students whose college education had been interrupted by the war, and who now were preparing to graduate and find their places in the business world.

But Wilkinson's most significant and enduring contribution to the life of the University came with the founding of the Graduate School of Business Administration. In the immediate postwar period, it became apparent to the more far-sighted members of the state's academic and business communities that Virginia required an institution of higher learning for finance and business students who wished to pursue their education beyond the undergraduate level. For too long, many of the state's best financial minds had been forced to go outside Virginia for professional training (as had Harvie himself), and there was increasing concern that the South was losing the top executive talent in each rising generation to corporations headquartered in other regions of the country.

As his son Jay looks on, Harvie turns over the check
from the successful 1952 Community Chest fund-raising
drive to chest president Horace A. Gray.

J. Harvie Wilkinson, Jr., executive vice president of the State-Planters Bank and Trust Company of Richmond,
moderates panel discussion at the finance forum presented by the bank for the Junior League of Richmond.
Left to right: Fielding L. Williams, attorney; L. Burwell Gunn, vice president and trust officer of State-Planters;
R. W. Wiltshire, vice president of the Home Beneficial Life Insurance Company of Richmond; Mr. Wilkinson;
Mrs. Anton C. Adams, Mrs. G. Gilmer Minor, Jr., and Miss Virginia Wellford, members of the league; and
Miss Virginia O. Valentine, advertising manager of the bank, who directed the forum.

The South had long lagged behind the North and Midwest in industrial development and the formation of capital, and in the minds of many financial and industrial executives, the absence of a first-rate graduate business school merely exacerbated the disparity. As Wilkinson aptly pointed out, the problem was a dearth not only of readily available credit, but of manpower and leadership; indeed, Harvie argued strongly that the South's "population drain is the greatest factor with which it has to contend":

> Probably the greatest challenge to the South today is the prevention of the loss of so much of its mental topsoil. Over the past twenty years, migration from the Southeastern states has been in substantial part drawn from its vigorous and dynamic leaders in business. These individuals could not find within their own section their technical business education and their field of opportunity.

At that time, there was no exclusive graduate school of business in the entire South, nor were there any such schools affiliated with a state university anywhere in the nation. Nevertheless, if a new institution were to be established in the South, the University of Virginia appeared to be the logical site. The University enjoyed a long tradition of excellence in business education — it had offered business economy courses as early as 1826, and the undergraduate school of commerce and business administration had been in operation since 1920 — and many of its graduates with business majors were eager to pursue their studies further and acquire an advanced degree.

In the summer of 1946, therefore, the faculty of the Schools of Economics and Commerce at the University unanimously endorsed a report calling for the establishment of a graduate school of business in Charlottesville. Copies of the report were sent to a few select members of the Virginia business community, including J. Harvie Wilkinson, Jr. In his reply to the faculty, Wilkinson strongly endorsed the concept of such a project, and urged the University to "develop a real Business School on the basis of the experience and groundwork you have so effectively laid." "That end is a very warm hope of mine," he added, "and I will do the best I can to help in any way we determine an alumnus could be effective." For a start, Harvie offered his suggestions for three "ingredients" which he felt should be incorporated into the philosophy of the new school: first, it should be a national school; second, that it should inculcate moral principles in its students; and third, that it should have a "peculiar applicability" to the business needs of Virginia and the South at large. In other words, Harvie did not wish the school to be merely a "Little Harvard"; as he later put it, he believed the school should "find a niche…embodying the moral values and the other spiritual essentials that comprise the University of Virginia. That is the path to take."

The prospect of establishing a graduate business school touched Harvie so deeply that he wrote again to the faculty on February 25, 1947, recommending that they develop a specific proposal to "assist the President and Rector at such time as they undertake the endowment drive for the business school… It seems to me that we have a golden opportunity here to develop a cause unique." Accordingly, University President Colgate Darden formed a twenty-four member Steering Committee of prominent businessmen throughout the state to plan and conduct a campaign for funds for the school's initial endowment. Not surprisingly, Harvie Wilkinson was elected vice-chairman of the committee.

Members of the University of Virginia Graduate School of Business Sponsors Committee at a meeting in December, 1952. From left to right on the front row are Colgate W. Darden, Jr., President of the University of Virginia; Henry E. McWane, Chairman of the Sponsors Committee and J. Harvie Wilkinson, Jr., Vice Chairman.

At the committee's first meeting on November 8, 1948, Wilkinson defined the objectives of the proposed school as the training of business statesmen from all over the United States, with particular emphasis on Virginia and the South. The motto for the school, he suggested, might be "to serve Virginia business better." To get the ball rolling, the committee voted to set a goal of raising $1.5 million from Virginia business interests. If they proved unable to obtain at least $1,000,000, the project would be scuttled and all gifts returned to their donors.

For the next three years, Harvie and his colleagues on the executive committee — aided by President Darden — traversed the state tirelessly, encouraging contributions and testifying before the appropriations committees of the Virginia legislature. Progress was painfully slow, but by the end of 1952 they had obtained $1,028,176, an amount which was deemed sufficient for the initial endowment. Subsequently, the state government appropriated an amount equal to the income from this endowment to cover the operating costs of the school for the first two years.

Yet Wilkinson's work was not yet done. Once the school became a reality, Harvie agreed to serve as vice-president of its newly-established Board of Trustees.

Harvie, Vice President of the Board of Trustees, Dr. Charles C. Abbott, Dean, Graduate School of Business and Irving D. Dawes, Secretary of the Sponsors Committee, meeting in Richmond in 1957 to raise funds to finance research and better salaries for highly qualified faculty.

As they viewed it, the Trustees' task was to rally support beyond mere financial contributions among the business community and the public at large for the entire educational program at the school (which, in 1973 was named in honor of former University President Colgate Darden). As Harvie himself put it, "The gift of substance without self, great though it be, will lack the luster which the spirit of the giver can alone bring to our common cause." Moreover, the Trustees met each month with the Faculty Committee of the University "to review and discuss presentations from the deans of other graduate business schools," to inaugurate the search procedure for the first dean of the school, establish a student loan program, and select an agent to administer the endowment fund.

These activities on behalf of the Darden School represented an immense investment of time, but Harvie was only too glad to use this opportunity to further the interests of the University. At the same time, he was cheering on his alma mater with equal enthusiasm in another, more prosaic fashion. Although he had never been known as an athlete during his undergraduate days (save for his tenure as captain of the cross-country team), Harvie remained an avid football fan, and each autumn he would spend as many Saturday afternoons as possible rooting for the University's gridiron team. When his elder son, Jay, was four years old, Harvie and Letitia began taking him to Scott Stadium to watch the games in person.

On June 1 the following year (1949), Harvie and Letitia's second son, Lewis Porter Wilkinson, was born, and when Lewis reached the magic age of four he, too, joined the weekly autumnal pilgrimages to Charlottesville. The family would pack a box lunch, take along some Coca-Colas and Harvie's special martinis for Mom and Dad, along with a thermos of coffee, and have a picnic behind the Colonnade Club. Then they would stroll around the Grounds before and after the game, while Harvie pointed out the places that had meant so much to him during his student days. There was little talking during the games, however, because Jay and Lewis quickly learned that their father took his football seriously.

Unfortunately, the Wilkinson boys' childhood years coincided with the football team's infamous 28-game losing streak. "It was just agony," Jay recalled, "but we kept going. We took that long drive up to Charlottesville on Route 250, just to watch them lose. But that was what loyalty was all about." At the games, Harvie bought his sons programs so they could learn the names of all the players, including the interior linemen,

Harvie with his infant son, Lewis Porter Wilkinson.

and the subject of University of Virginia football provided father and sons with a common interest and a valuable bond.

Harvie's relationship with his sons was certainly more casual than his experiences with his own father, though there remained a certain degree of formality between the generations. He would often take the boys to see the Richmond Virginians, a minor-league baseball team (part of the Triple A International League), or toss the football with Jay and Lewis in the yard after the family returned from church on Sunday afternoons, despite the fact that Harvie sometimes forgot to change out of his shirt and tie first. From time to time he would also take the boys fishing at nearby Custis Pond. Harvie used the occasion of one such fishing trip to explain to Jay all about the birds and bees. When he suggested a similar excursion to Lewis several years later, however, Lewis replied, "Dad, I'd love to go down there and catch some fish. But as for knowing about sex, the boys in the neighborhood filled me in long ago, and what they didn't tell me, Jay did."

Jay Wilkinson hands Richmond Virginians first baseman Johnny Jaciuk a $50 savings bond from State-Planters for hitting the first home run over the bank's sign on the right field fence at Parker field.

Ever since his father died, Harvie had remained especially close to his widowed mother, who still resided in Richmond with several of her sisters. Harvie spoke with Mrs. Wilkinson nearly every day, and took Letitia and the boys to visit her at least once a week, until her death in June 1952. He also acted as a surrogate father to his two nephews, the sons of his sister Marie Wilkinson Fitzgerald, after their own father died at an early age. Harvie made certain that both boys were well provided for, and that they both received a good education. One of Marie's sons, Harvie Fitzgerald, recalls that when he reached the proper age, his uncle Harvie offered to pay for either two years of prep school away from home, or four years of private school in Richmond. He chose to attend Woodberry for two years, and subsequently entered the University of Virginia, where the financial costs of his four years of undergraduate studies were also borne by his uncle. Later, after completing his military service in the United States Coast Guard, Harvie Fitzgerald entered the University of Virginia Graduate School of Business Administration and become a member of its first graduating class in 1957.

Like many of his contemporaries, Harvie Wilkinson thrived on a highly-structured routine in his family life. When he returned home in the evenings, he always reserved the first thirty minutes for quiet moments and a cocktail alone with Letitia, to relax and share the events of the day. Evening meals were, by current standards, rather formal affairs; Harvie invariably wore a coat and tie for dinner, and occasionally for breakfast, too. Such was the air of authority he projected that in each family room, there was always a seat that was indisputably Harvie's. "When he was absent from the dining room table, or if he wasn't home by the time we gathered in the library," noted Jay, "I would not have dared to sit in that seat."

Harvie was not the sort of man who mixed easily and casually with children, and yet his sons knew that "there was always so much love there." He often said to Letitia, "The bank absorbs so much of my time, I wonder if the boys know how much I love them — that they come first with me." Since their time together in the evenings was limited by early bedtimes and the voluminous reading material Harvie often brought home from the office to read — the briefcase set down by his special chair in the library was always bulging with reports and newspapers — Harvie, Jay, and Lewis enjoyed especially their time together during summer vacations, particularly their trips to Virginia Beach and Woodberry Forest. Wilkinson's First Rule of Summer Vacationing was to always take off two weeks at a time, so he could spend the first week unwinding from the pressures of the bank, and still have the second week to enjoy sheer, unadulterated fun. "Only in the second week do you really recharge your batteries," Harvie repeatedly stated.

One of the rare exceptions to this rule occurred when the family took a vacation through the western United States. Before the trip began, Harvie discovered that he needed to catch up on some work at the office, and so he managed to miss the "rough and tumble" parts of the journey, catching up with Letitia and the boys only after they had reached the more civilized environs of San Francisco and Los Angeles.

As the boys grew older, the family occasionally vacationed in Nantucket, and in 1964 took a trip to Mexico. During the latter trip, Harvie and Letitia found themselves longing for a quiet late-afternoon respite around the hotel swimming pool, though Jay and Lewis were still full of boisterous, youthful energy. As the boys splashed and horsed around in the pool, Letitia turned to Harvie and said, "You know, Harvie, the boys are

Letitia, Lewis, Harvie and Jay at Virginia Beach.

getting older now. I expect this is the last trip they'll ever want to take with us." And Harvie replied drily, "I don't know about that, but it's the last trip I'll ever want to take with them."

In the winter, while the boys attended school, Harvie and Letitia usually went away for a week or two by themselves, often to Jamaica or Florida. And every year at Christmas, starting in 1958 when the family moved into their new house at 109 Kennondale Lane, Harvie and Letitia threw a special holiday party for their close friends and family. They began by inviting only a few couples, who brought along their children, too, but as the years went by and the families grew, so did the size of the party. "We finally ended up with three generations of the same little group," recalled Letitia.

Jay, Letitia, Harvie and Lewis in Mexico, 1964.

Daisy Hicks, the Wilkinsons' long-time housekeeper
and friend.

The culinary highlights of the occasion always included spiced beef (which was prepared
by soaking the meat in brine for several months in the fall) and the coconut cake baked
by Daisy Hicks, the Wilkinson family's housekeeper and cook, who has been loved and
respected as a member of the family for almost fifty years.

Both Jay and Lewis enjoyed a remarkable camaraderie with their father. Despite
the pressures of his hectic schedule, Harvie always managed to be near his sons to counsel
them when they faced major decisions in their lives. Because he kept his own thoughts
firmly focused on the future — not just one year, but twenty or even thirty years ahead —
his advice to his sons tended to focus on long-range considerations. For instance, when
Jay was about twelve years old, Harvie decided that he should spend eight weeks of
summer camp in New Hampshire. He understood how much Jay loved Virginia, and he
knew that Jay would probably want to spend the rest of his life in the South; yet Harvie
also realized how important it was for Jay to acquire a broader perspective — to see the

world from another viewpoint — and he thought an extended stay in the Northeast might be especially helpful.

In the same fashion, Harvie suggested that Jay leave the comfortable confines of St. Christopher's School in Richmond to attend Lawrenceville School, near Princeton, New Jersey. The plan seems to have worked, for Jay elected to take his undergraduate degree at Yale University in New Haven, Connecticut, before returning to study law at the University of Virginia. During his senior year at Yale, Jay completed most of the research for his classic study of modern Virginia politics, *Harry Byrd and the Changing Face of Virginia Politics, 1945-1966* (published by the University Press of Virginia in 1968), which he dedicated to his father. Whenever Jay came home for a visit, he and Harvie would sit for hours discussing the most recent developments in state politics, or the latest sports scores. (Harvie continued to root for the New York baseball Giants long after they had moved to San Francisco.)

On the other hand, Harvie always saw his younger son, Lewis, as a more adventurous type who might benefit from staying closer to home, and so Lewis attended St. Christopher's and the University of Virginia, before launching his own business career with Philip Morris, Inc. in London and New York. Harvie frequently said how much he envied Lewis' expertise in the ever-expanding fields of technology, electronics, photography, and computers, and he would often say, "Lewis can fix anything. He's the only one in this house who can."

By the time Jay and Lewis were old enough to attend prep school, the McGuire School, sadly, was no longer in existence. Financial problems — in large measure the result of Mr. McGuire's reluctance to press his less wealthy students for payment of their tuition — had caused the school to close in the early 1940s. Such was the measure of Harvie Wilkinson's dedication to McGuire's memory, however, that when the school building was razed, he purchased some of the bricks and later used them in the construction of his home on Kennondale Lane. Further, Harvie and other McGuire School alumni raised contributions to establish a special fund at St. Christopher's School in memory of their late beloved headmaster, John Peyton McGuire III.

But Harvie never pressured either of his sons to follow a career in banking. For him, the essential consideration was always that an individual contribute to society according to his or her interests and talents, though he deemed some form of contribution absolutely essential. He expected much of others because he expected so much of himself. Two things that Harvie absolutely would not tolerate were indolence — especially unused talent — and selfishness. "The waste of talent to me is really the unforgivable sin," he once wrote, "because the world is inevitably the poorer. Why are we put here if it is not to plow back into society the capacities we have and thereby enrich our contemporaries, as well as the oncoming generations?" □

III

TOWARD A UNITED VIRGINIA

Banks should be operated with full
appreciation of the fact that they are
timeless institutions.

— J. HARVIE WILKINSON, JR.

In the fifth century B.C., the Athenian philosopher-statesman Pericles claimed that his remarkably well-governed city-state owed its preeminence to the fact that "our citizens attend both to public and private duties, and do not allow absorption in their own affairs to interfere with their knowledge of their city." Certainly few citizens of Richmond could have matched Harvie Wilkinson's record of civic involvement in those first years after World War II. It was true that Wilkinson believed that a successful businessman owed a debt to the community that had supported him. It was equally true, as Harvie freely acknowledged, that "over a long life one gets an abiding and deep satisfaction from contributing to those causes and institutions that make for a better and richer community, richer in the educational and cultural opportunities that have been afforded the generations now living and those yet unborn."

It is also fair to say that Harvie Wilkinson recognized that State-Planters Bank would benefit from his involvement in community affairs. Accordingly, he strove to expand his commitments outside the bank and constantly urged his colleagues at State-Planters to contribute their talents in a similar fashion. "As a representative of the bank," he declared, "your personal involvement speaks well for the bank and enhances its image in the community. At the same time, involvement in civic affairs provides you with a base of intelligence and knowledge of the community which is indispensable to the bank in making sure that it is providing up-to-date services in keeping with changing times. Your involvement will help keep the bank aware of the community's needs and thus enable it to improve its role as a corporate citizen in enhancing the economic and social life of the community." Everyone — the community, the bank, and the individual — benefitted from the exercise of responsible corporate citizenship. It was not surprising, therefore, that Harvie willingly loaned his time and talents to a myriad of civic and corporate organizations in the postwar decades.

One of Harvie's most cherished causes — and one to which, as he astutely recognized, the future of State-Planters was clearly tied — was the state government's effort in the postwar era to develop the industrial base of Virginia. As Governor William Tuck admitted in 1948, "That we are not making the most of some of our natural and human resources is obvious." In an attempt to bolster Virginia's bid to attract new businesses and to encourage the expansion of existing firms, the General Assembly approved that same year the establishment of an Advisory Council on the Virginia Economy. Given Harvie's interest in encouraging a progressive attitude among the state's business leaders, it is not surprising that he was among the dozen prominent political and economic leaders selected for membership on the Council's executive committee.

Simultaneously, Harvie also served as a director of the Richmond Chamber of Commerce, and as a member of the Board of Commissioners of the city's Sinking Fund. Even Harvie had his limits, however; when the City Council in 1951 again pressed him to run for a seat on that body, he regretfully found it necessary to decline the honor because of the press of other duties, despite one Councilman's prediction that Wilkinson "could be elected unanimously, if he would serve."

In the corporate financial community, Harvie accepted a wide range of responsibilities within the banking profession. Long active in the affairs of the American Bankers Association, Harvie was appointed a member of both the Association's executive and research councils in 1952. That same year, he was named to the economic policy committee of the United States Chamber of Commerce, a group which developed studies and recommendations that were used in formulating basic chamber policies and preparing testimony for congressional committees. Somehow, amid the press of all his other obligations, Harvie also found time to serve on the boards of numerous well-known national and local corporations, including Philip Morris, Inc., Richmond Television Corporation, Miller & Rhoads, Inc., Richmond Newspapers, Dan River Mills, and the Commonwealth Natural Gas Corporation.

Readers of the Richmond newspapers soon grew accustomed to seeing Harvie's photograph — with his hair invariably neatly parted in the middle — on the pages of the business and metropolitan news sections. Always a meticulous dresser, Harvie had by this time accumulated an extensive wardrobe that was the envy of his associates. "He had the most amazing variety of suits and jackets," marvelled Virginius Dabney, who once heard Harvie complain that a dry cleaner had misplaced eight of his winter suits. "Eight winter suits!" repeated Dabney. "I don't think I even owned eight different suits in twenty years!" Clearly Harvie had come a long way, sartorially speaking, since those dark Depression days when he owned only few drab gray suits.

Despite Harvie's enthusiastic dedication to the needs and interests of the outside community, the growth and well-being of State-Planters always remained his top priority. And in the immediate postwar period, the bank had great need of his vision and tireless energy. After essentially treading water during the war, the bank had emerged from the difficult readjustment period of 1946-47 in a relatively strong position. In 1939, for instance, deposits had totalled nearly $57 million, and net income had been $420,000; by 1947, deposits had risen to more than $140 million, and net income to nearly $700,000. But the United States economy had been through an unprecedented decade of depressed business activity in the 1930s, followed by four years of total war, and if the postwar era promised to bring a return to economic normalcy, it was not at all clear to most expert observers precisely what normalcy was.

Certainly most bankers, especially those in the conservative South, were in no mood to take any unnecessary chances that might jeopardize the welcome and long overdue recovery. Yet Virginia in the early 1950s stood on the brink of a prolonged period of vigorous economic expansion, though only a few far-seeing corporate and political leaders understood just how revolutionary the change would be. If the proper groundwork were laid, new industrial and service corporations would be entering Virginia, and established firms would seek to expand their operations, and all would require extensive reserves of capital.

Since corporate lending was, after all, State-Planters' primary field of operations, the bank responded positively, albeit cautiously to the rising demand for credit. In the spring of 1951, State-Planters' loans reached an all-time high of $54 million. The bank still enjoyed a major share of the business clients in town, numbering among its customers such prestigious local corporations as Miller & Rhoads and Southern States — whom State-Planters had steadfastly supported during the dark days of the Depression — along with national corporations like General Motors and Ford that regularly employed lines of credit with a host of regional banks across the country. State-Planters was also one of the nation's leading financiers of the tobacco leaf production industry, providing services to Philip Morris, Inc., and Universal Leaf Tobacco, among others.

The bank's Trust Department, too, under the direction of L. Burwell Gunn, was prospering and setting new records for activity and the historically strong State-Planters Correspondent Bank Department, under the leadership of James W. Rawles, retained its position as the largest such operation in Virginia. But mortgage loans remained anathema to the bank's officers, largely because of their dismal experience during the Depression; nor was President Harry Augustine terribly eager to make automobile loans. As far as Augustine was concerned, if a customer could not afford to pay cash for a new car, he probably should not buy one. Thus, while the bank did enter into the field of consumer loans in a modest way, it did so with a marked lack of enthusiasm. Such matters were better left to finance companies and savings and loans.

In 1949, State-Planters had inaugurated, largely on Harvie Wilkinson's initiative, a management training program for college graduates to accompany the expanded recruitment effort that the bank's personnel committee — again, under Harvie's prodding — had recommended. Often Harvie and Moncure "Pat" Patteson, who by that time was a vice president and the cashier of the bank, represented State-Planters on recruiting trips. Their interview methodology was not always entirely orthodox, as a University of Virginia senior named Richard Dilworth discovered when the pair visited Charlottesville in the spring of 1951. After suffering through a conventional career interview with a representative of a staid and rather stuffy New York banking firm, Dilworth was somewhat taken aback by the jocularity (not to say downright foolishness) displayed by the State-Planters executives:

When I walked into the room for my appointment with State-Planters, here were Harvie Wilkinson and Pat Patteson, both of whom were men of short stature. Probably both were slightly taller than I was, but not by a great deal. And when I walked in, Harvie said, "Here's one our size!" Somehow in the ensuing hilarity, they insisted that I stand back-to-back with them, so they could assure the other that each was taller than I was.

Significantly, Wilkinson asked Dilworth — after the laughter had died down — if he possessed imagination, a quality which Harvie certainly valued more highly than his traditionalist colleagues.

State-Planters did, in fact, offer Dilworth a position, and he accepted and became one of the four members of that year's management training group. Upon his arrival in Richmond, Dilworth discovered that the atmosphere at the bank, which then numbered perhaps 300 employees, was remarkably informal for an establishment of its size. "It was a really wonderful institution," Dilworth recalled, "and not just as a bank. There were an awful lot of nice people there. And nearly all these people, even the senior officers, were called by their first names, which was a little unusual."

On Christmas Eve, 1952, the State-Planters board of directors named Harvie Wilkinson executive vice president, a new position created especially for him. The promotion marked Wilkinson as the leading contender for the presidency of State-Planters when Harry Augustine retired, and appears to have been designed to involve Harvie more deeply in the management of the bank's activities outside the investment department.

At the time, many officers and employees of State-Planters seemed surprised that the board had chosen Wilkinson to be the heir apparent. Harvie had spent virtually his entire career at the bank in the investment department, while the lifeblood of State-Planters — and the traditional training ground for its top offices — had always been the credit side of its operations. Moreover, Harvie was considerably more intellectual and more sophisticated than many of his colleagues, and some of them found him somewhat distant, if not aloof.

Yet Harry Augustine had recommended the forty-six year-old Wilkinson precisely because Harvie possessed that rare combination of intellectual and leadership qualities. Augustine recognized that the banking business was changing and changing swiftly, and he knew that Wilkinson possessed the vision, breadth of knowledge, and aggressiveness to guide State-Planters into the latter half of the twentieth century.

Harvie had never been shy about offering advice to his colleagues at State-Planters, but his promotion appeared to encourage him to increase the pace and range of his recommendations, until the flow of memoranda from his office on all sorts of topics became a veritable blizzard of paper. Although he certainly saw no shortage of tasks that required attention, the greatest challenge, for Harvie, lay in awakening his colleagues at State-Planters to the opportunities that lay before them. Instead of allowing the bank to rest upon its laurels, or continue in its comfortable and traditional path, Harvie constantly and aggressively urged his colleagues to explore new avenues of growth. "Virginia stands for conservatism," he acknowledged, "and Virginia has conservative banks. That does not mean that Virginia cannot have progressive banks."

"Building the bank" became a constant theme of Harvie's messages. He urged all the officers and the entire staff of the bank to become deeply involved in attracting new business to State-Planters, and he provided them with bits of specific advice on how to get the job done. "The secret of selling is as follows," he wrote. "It is better to spend one hour of time with a man who makes the decision than to spend ten visits of six minutes each with the man who has to seek approval." Or, since the task of building the bank necessarily extended into the evening hours as well, Harvie (who loved to combine business with good food and fine wine) reminded his colleagues that "It is better to entertain the decision-maker at a fine $10 dinner than it is to entertain the one who has to seek approval at five $2 lunches."

Few things irritated Wilkinson more than the sight of two State-Planters officials chatting with each other at a social gathering. "If he caught a bank person talking to another bank person at a social function," recalled Jack Jennings, who later became president of State-Planters, "he would say, 'There's no money to be made doing that. Go out and find customers and talk to them.'"

Harvie's own performance in attracting new customers set lofty standards for the rest of the State-Planters executive corps. After the bank began keeping records of individual producers of new trust business in the 1950s, it was discovered Harvie brought in over $32 million dollars in trust accounts — almost twice that of the nearest

Harry Augustine and Wilfred Roper sign the agreement merging State-Planters and the Bank of Commerce and Trusts.

associate — over the following twenty years. That total did not include the millions of dollars of commercial business that he produced, of course, or the endowment account of the University of Virginia which Harvie and his colleagues were able to obtain.

As the pace of economic expansion quickened in the mid-1950s, the corresponding need for additional capital increased apace. In March 1955, State-Planters took a significant step toward meeting that need when it announced that it had begun negotiations to merge with the Bank of Commerce and Trusts. The latter bank, founded in 1905, was less than one-fifth the size of State-Planters in terms of deposits, but it possessed a strong capital position and a presence in south Richmond, which State-Planters lacked. Moreover, the combined assets (approximately $207 million) and deposits ($195 million) of the two banks made the new institution — known as the State-Planters Bank of Commerce and Trusts — officially the largest bank in the state.

"The growth of business in Virginia requires an increase in the lending ability on the part of the banks," declared Harry Augustine in announcing the plans for the merger.

With a total capitalization in excess of $14 million, and a lending limit of $1.2 million to any one borrower, State-Planters now was well placed to meet that need. When the merger became final in early 1956, Augustine remained president of the new bank, while Wilfred Roper, former head of the Bank of Commerce, assumed the chairmanship. For the time being, Harvie Wilkinson retained his position as executive vice president.

Yet as early as 1957, the bank found itself hard-pressed to meet the rising demand for commercial credit. In the autumn of that year, outstanding loans at State-Planters reached an all-time high of $94 million, sending the bank's gross operating income to record levels. The brief but sharp dip in economic activity that marked the final two years of the Eisenhower administration eased the credit crunch slightly, but only temporarily.

On January 9, 1958, the board of directors of State-Planters Bank of Commerce and Trusts elected Harvie Wilkinson to succeed Harry Augustine as president of the bank. Augustine, whose health had been failing, was named chairman of the board, and Wilfred Roper became vice chairman of the board and chairman of the executive committee.

One of Harvie's first acts as president of State-Planters was to open negotiations for a merger with the Citizens National Bank of Petersburg. In March 1959, the two institutions formally announced their decision to unite, thereby providing State-Planters with a presence in Petersburg (approximately 25 miles south of Richmond) and adding another $1.4 million of capital funds to the bank. According to Wilkinson, who was named president and chief executive officer of the merged bank (still known as State-Planters Bank of Commerce and Trusts), the move was designed to help provide better and more efficient services to businesses and individuals in the Richmond-Petersburg-Hopewell triangle. "As the boundaries of the three cities inevitably grow together," he explained, "the merged bank will be in a position to offer services in line with the needs of the growing population and the expanding companies within the area."

And the economy of the region clearly was in a period of widespread expansion. Reynolds Metals had constructed a $10 million office building in Henrico County and a $5.5 million plant in Chesterfield County; the A. H. Robins Company, headed by another McGuire School alumnus, Claiborne Robins, was well on its way to becoming one of the nation's leading pharmaceutical firms; and Wheat, First Securities — headed

Harvie and Benjamin T. Kinsey approving the merger of the
Citizens National Bank of Petersburg with State-Planters.

by Harvie Wilkinson's good friend, James C. Wheat — had begun its rise to dominance
among investment banking firms in the Southeast. Late in 1959, Philip Morris opened a
major new research center along the recently-opened Richmond-Petersburg Turnpike.
That same year, Richmond's two largest department stores, Miller & Rhoads and
Thalhimers, announced plans to establish their first outlets in the suburbs. By the end of
1959, State-Planters' assets totalled over $233 million, shattering yet another record.

Richmond was also enjoying a cultural renaissance during this period, fueled in
large measure by the heightened economic vitality of central Virginia. The Richmond
Opera Group, chartered in 1946, expanded its programs of operettas, concerts, and
pageants in the Lyric Theater, and in 1957 the Richmond Symphony, a victim of tight
budgets during the Depression of the 1930s, was revived to the delight of classical music
lovers in the city. Further, the Virginia Museum of Fine Arts expanded its quarters to
house its growing collection of exquisite paintings, sculpture, jewels, and historical
artifacts, accompanied by frequent performances of drama, music, and dance.

Monroe Park after a tornado cut a path of destruction
through Richmond in 1951.

Richmond's venerable streetcar system already had disappeared in 1949, replaced
by modern buses. Motorists wishing to cross the James at the western edge of town found
a wider, more modern Huguenot Bridge in place of the old one-lane Westham span. And
the city fathers had replaced more than a thousand of the trees in Byrd and Monroe Parks
that had been uprooted during the famous tornado of June 1951.

With the exception of a few relatively minor incidents, racial relations in
Richmond remained excellent, as the city made steady progress toward integration in
hotels, restaurants, theaters, and retail stores. After surveying the situation in detail in
1962, the *Washington Post* wrote its conclusion in a headline: "Richmond Quietly Leads
Way in Race Relations." In a similar vein, *New York Times* journalist Arthur Krock
described Richmond two years later as "a model for every town, city, and county in the
United States."

Certainly Harvie Wilkinson welcomed all these signs of economic, cultural, and
social progress. As president of State-Planters, Wilkinson focused on the overall direction

of State-Planters, and generally refrained from excessive interference with the day-to-day operations of the bank, especially on the credit side; his vision already was focused on a plan to ensure the long-term growth and stability of the bank. Harvie did, however, feel an affinity for big business, partly because of his years of service on numerous corporate boards, and he had long made a practice of personally calling upon State-Planters' major corporate customers in the New York metropolitan area.

When he was in New York, Harvie usually arranged to meet one of the bank's clients each night for dinner. (He even kept a tuxedo in Manhattan especially for formal occasions.) Typically, Harvie would visit the restaurant he had selected in the afternoon, introduce himself to the maitre d' (and tip him handsomely), select a table, and meet the waiter and busboys, tipping them as well. Then, when he arrived with his guest for dinner, Harvie would be met at the door with a warm greeting — "Ah, Mr. Wilkinson, how nice to have you back. Your table is ready"— and excellent service throughout the meal.

Harvie was not, however, particularly interested in the nuts and bolts of the commercial lending process, and since the bank had two outstanding loan officers in vice presidents Carlisle R. Davis (who had been at State-Planters since 1921) and Edward F. Gee (who joined the bank in 1929, the same year as Harvie), Wilkinson felt confident in delegating substantial authority to them.

Indeed, Harvie believed that the entire bank was, in the late 1950s, "in the process of shifting from a high degree of centralization of decisions to decentralization of decisions," and he claimed that State-Planters would be far better served "if the people who are concerned with the supervisory, administrative, policy-forming functions at the various levels of the official staff will focus on and attack this problem." Accordingly, he recommended that his officers focus increasingly upon "planning, organizing, administering, and following through," while spending less time at their technical specialties — lending, investing, managing trusts, and so forth.

As a corollary to this management philosophy, Harvie adopted what he called the "Completed Staff Work" theory. Perhaps the most well-known of all the memoranda that he promulgated during his tenure at the bank, the Completed Staff Work principle required subordinates to study a problem thoroughly and decide upon a single proposed action before presenting it to a staff officer or section head. "Do not worry your chief or department head with long explanations and memoranda," Harvie warned. "Your views should be placed before him in finished form so that he can make them his views simply by signing his name. Your chief should merely approve or disapprove." Harvie acknowledged that this procedure "may result in more work for the staff members, but it results in more freedom for the chief. This is as it should be." And so it should, especially if the chief had as little patience for endless recitations of minor details as did Harvie Wilkinson.

June 1, 1957

The following summary of "Completed Staff Work" summarizes well my ideas on the subject, and I ask that you commit to memory the contents. It is my purpose to take action principally after completed staff work has been finished and not before, and this is the way that problems should be presented:

"Completed Staff Work" is the study of a problem, and presentation of a solution, by a staff officer or section head, in such form that all that remains to be done on the art of the head of the department is to indicate his approval or disapproval of the COMPLETED ACTION.

"The words 'completed action' are emphasized because the more difficult the problem is, the more the tendency is to present the problem to the department head in piece-meal fashion.

"It is your duty as a member of the staff to work out the details. You should not consult your chief in the determination of those details, no matter how perplexing they may be. You may and should consult other staff members. The product, whether it involves the pronouncement of a new policy or affects an established one, should, when presented to the department head or chief for approval or disapproval, be worked out in FINISHED FORM.

"The impulse which often comes to the inexperienced staff officer or section head to ask the chief what to do recurs more often when the problem is difficult. It is accompanied by a feeling of mental frustration. It is so easy to ask the chief what to do, and it appears so easy for him to answer. Resist that impulse. You will succumb to it only if you do not know your job. It is your job to advise or suggest to your chief what he should do, not ask him what you should do. He needs answers and suggestions, not questions. Your job is to study, budget and investments, helping the institution through a difficult period of budgetary restraints, and keeping alive its vital cultural mission, which he defined as "improving the tastes of the broad community and enhancing a love of beauty, of that which is good and ennobling. These are indeed needed ingredients in our commercial and frenetic world." Harvie's own tastes in art ran toward the traditional, though he was quite open-minded about abstract, non-representational works. Not surprisingly, he was always willing to voice his opinions about what he liked and what he did not.

The following month, Governor Holton appointed Wilkinson to the State Council of Higher Education, the body established by the General Assembly in 1956 to oversee the Commonwealth's system of colleges and universities. For the first sixteen years of its existence, the eleven-member Council had not enjoyed substantial influence; but beginning in 1972 — coincidental with Harvie's appointment — the state mounted a major study of the Council's role, with an eye toward increasing its responsibilities for planning, coordinating, and regulating Virginia's programs of higher education.

Subsequent legislation passed by the legislature in 1974, at the start of Mills Godwin's second term as Governor, provided the Council with a greatly enhanced status, and the authority "to promote a sound, progressive system of higher education, and to ensure that the money to fund that system was equitably distributed." Specifically, the Council was charged with the responsibility to approve enrollment projections, set guidelines for budgets and make financial recommendations to the governor and the General Assembly, to approve all new degree programs, to advise on the creation of any new campuses, and to carry out whatever studies the governor or legislature deemed necessary.

Given Harvie Wilkinson's lifelong devotion to the cause of education, his appointment to the Council was perhaps the capstone of his career in public service. During his first four-year term, Wilkinson's counsel and experience proved invaluable as the Council struggled to deal with the still-vexing issue of the integration of Virginia's colleges and universities. According to Gordon Davies, who assumed the directorship of the Council in 1976, Harvie attempted to navigate a middle course through this difficult matter. "On the one hand," recalled Davies, "he was entirely open to removing the vestiges of segregation. On the other hand, he found the wooden-handedness of [the federal] bureaucracy extremely annoying. He had a very strong commitment to the traditional sense of quality higher education, and he found much of what the federal bureaucracy would ask us to do either irrelevant or offensive to what his sense of quality was."

Rather than treat education as a political football, Wilkinson sought to increase the opportunities for first-rate education to all Virginians. For Harvie, education possessed tremendous potential for solving the nation's racial and social problems. As Davies explained,

> I remember him saying to me in that period, that the objective of this state (and others) had to be the creation of a strong and economically viable black middle class. Once we had created a strong and economically viable black middle class, many of the problems with which we were dealing would begin to sort themselves out, not along racial lines, but along socio-economic lines.

It was Harvie Wilkinson's firm belief that the Commonwealth's system of higher education should be precisely that — a system which, in his words, "implies a coordinated group of institutions supplying the varying needs of various people without the institutions trying to be 'all the same' to all the people," and without a "dilution of excellence." This was the direction in which Harvie strove to lead the Council during his second four-year term, including two years as Chairman of the Council. (He could have served a third year as Chairman, but Harvie elected to decline that honor because his eyesight had begun to fail, and he could no longer read as voluminously as he used to. Interestingly, since that date no one else has chosen to serve three years as chairperson of the Council; some have even explained their refusal by saying that "if Harvie thought two years was enough, then two was enough.")

As Chairman, Wilkinson attempted to ensure the opportunities for wider access that were manifest in the state's community college system and the regional four-year colleges such as George Mason, Old Dominion, and James Madison, while preserving the quality of those traditionally more selective institutions for which he felt a special affection: the University of Virginia, the College of William and Mary, and Virginia Polytechnic Institute. Further, Harvie was the first leader in Virginia to suggest that the undergraduate teacher education major be abolished. In testimony before the General Assembly in 1978, he recommended that all public school teachers should take liberal arts and science degrees, while acquiring education skills along the way. Harvie's words struck a responsive chord in many state political and academic officials across the state, and as the "back to basics" educational reform movement swept across the nation and Commonwealth in the following decade, the General Assembly adopted a modified version of Wilkinson's recommendations in 1986.

By the time his second term expired, Harvie had gone far toward turning the Council into a more professional education organization by bringing more academic personnel onto the line staff. His departure from the Council's board, however, did not end his involvement in the educational affairs of the Commonwealth. From time to time, the staff of the Council visited Harvie for advice, or for an introduction to a corporate executive or a state legislator. And at least every few months, Harvie invited Gordon Davies to lunch to discuss any problems that were currently facing Virginia's colleges.

At about the same time that Harvie stepped down from the Council of Higher Education, the seven Church Schools of the Diocese of Virginia decided to embark upon a major endowment campaign to create a central investment fund. The income from this fund was to be used as a challenge to the individual schools to raise additional endow-ment from their own alumni, parents, and friends. Clearly the schools would need dedicated leaders with considerable fund-raising experience and statewide contacts to coordinate this campaign, and Elise H. (Lee) Switz, who had recently joined the adminis-tration of the Church Schools recalls that Tom Boushall, the former chairman of the Bank of Virginia, recommended his longtime banking colleague Harvie Wilkinson for the job. "But," Boushall added with a twinkle in his eye, "don't tell him I sent you."

When the delegation from the Church Schools went to call on Harvie to ask his help, "he looked very serious and very stern, as if he were doing us a big favor" said Switz, but Harvie was only having a bit of fun. He told them that he would be pleased to serve, and the following day Harvie called Switz and asked her to lunch at UVB's offices. She informed him that there was no natural constituency for raising funds for the Church Schools as a group, and that the Diocese did not want to interfere with the normal flow of funds to individual schools. Undaunted, Harvie agreed to serve as chairman of the steering committee for the endowment fund, and — after Harvie persuaded his old friend James C. Wheat, Jr., to head the endowment committee — together he and Lee Switz set out on a series of trips across the state to encourage, prod, and inspire donors to contribute to the campaign.

James C. Wheat, Jr. and Harvie meet at
St. Christophers' School in 1984 to discuss progress
toward achieving the goal of the Church School's
Endowment campaign fund drive.

"Harvie did not like to fail," recalled Switz. "If he set out to do something, he did it." It was an opportunity for Harvie to renew old acquaintances, while contributing his energy and expertise to a cause he believed in deeply. "The future is now and the tomorrows of all times," he wrote. "In the process of raising endowment, we have propagated awareness of seven Schools that integrate rigorous discipline on the athletic field and in the classroom with the awareness that no talent or skill has value unless undergirded with the sinew of character. We need these Schools, and the need for quality education at the highest level has never been greater."

The campaign also gave Lee Switz a chance to get to know Harvie Wilkinson on a personal basis, and her insights into his character at the age of seventy-five are well worth noting. "He knew himself, and had a realistic appreciation of human nature," she explained. "He was a perfectionist, yet forgiving. His Christianity encompassed a system of clear, and to him God-given values, yet he understood ambiguity and paradox. He believed deeply in the doctrine of original sin, that human beings by nature are flawed. He also believed in redemption and forgiveness. He had a strong, well-disciplined intellect. He worked from his head, but at the same time was fully in touch with his emotions… I did not think he was egotistical, although I have heard him accused of arrogance at times; I saw him as serving God as he saw it, and as one of the most generous and modest people I have ever known."

Traditionally, education had been viewed as a nonpartisan area of public life in Virginia, where party affiliations were deemed less vital than the quality of civic leadership. For instance, Harvie — a longtime Democrat — had originally been appointed to the Council by a Republican governor, Linwood Holton. Yet the whole nature of politics in Virginia had already begun to change by this time, as the ideological lines between the parties blurred and, on occasion, virtually disappeared altogether. In the fall of 1973, for instance, Mills Godwin had campaigned for and won a second term as governor, this time as the standard-bearer of the Republican party. Godwin reached his decision to run reluctantly, persuaded by friends and associates who felt that the Democratic front-runner for the gubernatorial nomination, veteran Norfolk state senator Henry Howell, was far too liberal for their tastes.

Harvie Wilkinson was one of those who strongly urged Godwin to reenter the political fray in 1973. Actually, Harvie's conservative convictions had often led him to favor the G.O.P. presidential candidate in national elections, so his advocacy of Godwin's Republican candidacy should not have come as a surprise. For Wilkinson (and for numerous other business leaders), the governing factor in this case was his apprehension about the potential negative effects of Howell's election upon the state's economy. Naturally, Harvie was not reluctant to offer Godwin his own advice about the way the campaign should be run to ensure Howell's defeat. As Godwin recalled with a smile, "I met with Harvie at his request in Williamsburg, in a private office there. We had lunch, and he was urging me to do it, while at the same time telling me what I had to do in order to win. Which," he added, "I appreciated." Whether he followed Harvie's tactical advice or not, Godwin did emerge victorious, becoming the first individual in modern times to serve two terms as Governor of Virginia.

Whenever Harvie was in Richmond he spent at least five hours each weekday at his office at UVB, reviewing the progress of his personal investments on a special large-screen telewriter, staying current with events at the bank, and offering suggestions to his successors, though generally not in an intrusive manner. "Harvie never stopped offering advice," recalled Jack Jennings, "because he still had ideas, and his ideas were highly specific."

Sometimes Harvie adopted unconventional means to discuss matters with his successors. Late one afternoon, Jack Jennings was driving home along Cary Street, carefully conveying a supply of liquid refreshments on the front seat for a party he and his wife were hosting that evening. Observing an accident scene ahead at the intersection of Malvern and Cary, Jennings pulled his Lincoln over to the right and stopped along the side of the road. All of a sudden he looked in his rear-view mirror and, to his dismay, saw Harvie and his Buick bearing down upon him. Unable to stop in time, Harvie smashed into the rear of Jennings' car. Neither man was injured, though Harvie's Buick suffered considerable damage. (Jack confided later that he had been primarily concerned about the welfare of his evening's supply of liquor.)

As the two men sat in the police car providing details of the accident, an officer asked Jack how long he had been driving. "Well," Jennings answered, "I was a State Trooper back in 1938, so I know I was driving before then." "Mr. Wilkinson," the officer continued, "how long have you been driving?" "I say," Harvie replied dryly, "when did they invent the first car?"

After all the details had been cleared up and everyone was preparing to leave the scene, Harvie took Jack by the arm and said, "Jack, you had better get a good lawyer." "But Harvie," Jack protested, "anybody that runs into the back of someone else is automatically at fault." "You don't understand," Harvie insisted, with a twinkle in his eye. "My lawyer will be Justice Powell, and you won't stand a chance."

Both Jennings and Richard Tilghman, who became chairman and chief executive officer of UVB in August 1985, made a conscious effort to keep Harvie informed about the bank's activities and direction. In return, Harvie provided Jennings and Tilghman with the benefit of his considerable wisdom on the challenges of life at the top of a major financial corporation. In so doing, Harvie maintained a long-standing tradition in State-Planters and several of the other UVB affiliates, whereby senior officers maintained a high degree of accessibility to younger officers and even trainees, educating and motivating the rising generation of leadership.

"To me, Harvie possessed a great sense of the responsibility of a senior executive to reach down a generation or two and pump some knowledge into the people coming along," observed Tilghman. "I think Harvie made a conscious effort to communicate to several generations of management the kind of behavior an executive should exhibit. I'm quite sure that wasn't an accident. He probably saw that as part of his duty. Harvie clearly went to some trouble to educate people on how a chairman and a board should work together. He clearly put energy into teaching us to think long-term. And he asked questions that challenged you to be certain that you were thinking long-term."

Tilghman also discovered that Harvie represented an especially valuable source of advice on the role of a bank executive in the outside community. "I went to Harvie on more than one occasion for specific advice involving political or organizational matters outside the bank, where I knew he had a competence," noted Tilghman. "He was very interested, and personally furthered my involvement in a number of community activities, both social and civic. He had a deep belief that bankers had to be visibly involved in their community, in both social and civic organizations, and with the kind of people that would bring benefit to the bank as well."

Nearly every year during his retirement, Harvie and Letitia enjoyed an extended excursion abroad. In the summer of 1971, just one week after Harvie left UVB, the Wilkinsons took off for Europe with Paul and Bessie Sackett. The last stop in their journey was southern Portugal, and Harvie found the region absolutely enchanting. "Even on a rainy day, Harvie fell in love with the area," recalled Letitia, "because it was one of the unspoiled areas of Europe, and relatively inexpensive. So the next year, when we returned to Europe, he said he wanted to go there again." Over three days of whirl-wind negotiations with an expatriate British real estate agent, Harvie and Letitia purchased a site for a three-bedroom vacation home in an area known as Val de Lobo, decided on decorations, and concluded the financing arrangements. "Would that I had in Virginia," Harvie laughed, "an Englishman like that who would move things along as quickly."

For six years, Harvie and Letitia spent a month each autumn at their home in Val de Lobo. They often spent their days sight-seeing, touring through picturesque

Harvie and Letitia relax by the pool of their home at
Val de Lobo, Portugal.

Portugese villages, viewing historical sites — including the ports from which Henry the
Navigator launched so many expeditions during the fifteenth century — or visiting local
markets. After the first year, Harvie had a small swimming pool built in back of the
house, where he and Letitia and friends visiting from the States could enjoy leisurely
lunches of bread, cheese, wine, and fruit. In the evenings, revived and refreshed, Harvie
and his guests would go out for dinner at one of his favorite local taverns.

He and Letitia were able to furnish their Portugese home with beautiful hand-
crafted furniture, though one effort to import a work of Italian art to adorn the house
proved rather disconcerting. In one of their visits to Italy, Harvie and Letitia had purchased a painting that Harvie suspected was an undiscovered masterpiece. "Well,"
recalled Letitia, "the excitement was, how to get it there?"

Paul [Sackett] and Harvie knew they weren't going to cope with
carrying this thing on the plane, so they had our driver take it and have it
shipped. It arrived there ahead of us, and when we went to collect it from

the freight station, the Portugese officials said, "You owe us duty." They said it in Portugese, but we got the idea.

There were six of them standing around the painting. They looked at it, and they looked at each other, and they looked at us, and then they opened up the picture, and shook their heads. Finally they took our painting, which we thought was splendid — we all agreed it was an unknown masterpiece — put it on the scales, weighed it, and put the duty on according to the weight. That was quite disenchanting.

In whatever country he visited, Harvie had to find out what made the economy tick. If the cab driver at the airport displayed any knowledge of English Harvie's inquiries would begin immediately. Harvie and Letitia's trip to Japan in the early 1970s was particularly compelling in this quest for knowledge since their interest in Japan had been piqued in 1967 when a young Japanese exchange student, Mitsuyoshi Okano, lived with the Wilkinsons for six weeks. It was a delightful revelation for Harvie to later find out that Mitsu was from a banking family, The Suruga Bank having been founded by his great grandfather in 1895. During the Wilkinsons stay in Tokyo Mitsu's father, Kiichiro Okano, then president of The Suruga Bank, hosted a dinner party for Harvie and the head of The Fuji Bank. As a result of this visit, Harvie had a grand opportunity to learn everything he wanted to about Japan and he and Letitia developed a long lasting friendship with the Okano family, who later visited them in Richmond.

Among the more exotic journeys Harvie and Letitia embarked upon during these years were a safari across central and south Africa (where showers were taken in tents, using water brought from a nearby river by the native guides), a trip to Australia and the Far East, and a tour of the Balkans, during which a Romanian soldier brusquely informed them at the point of a bayonet that it was forbidden to walk along the sidewalk in front of the local Communist Party headquarters. (A similar tour of the Soviet Union was far more pleasant, with no such incidents or displays of hostility toward Western visitors.) Whenever possible, Harvie insisted that they return via London, so he could spend at least a day or two in his favorite lodgings at the Connaught Hotel.

Most of their winters were spent at their condominium in Delray Beach, Florida, where Harvie passed many lazy days asleep (while pretending to read a newspaper) under the shade of an umbrella in his favorite spot, known as "the philosopher's corner." Here,

With camera in hand and a good hat to keep the flies away, Harvie eagerly awaits his chance to see an Australian sheep farm near Melbourne.

Below: Vacations just wouldn't be complete without an occasional afternoon nap.

too, the prospect of a fine dinner revived Harvie in the evenings, sending him "off like a jackrabbit" in search of a gourmet meal. Unfortunately, Harvie was burdened by failing eyesight during the last years of his life, which made it impossible for him to maintain the tremendous volume of reading he had always enjoyed so much, though he was able to obtain a variety of recorded literature on cassette tapes from the Library of Congress, including Paul Johnson's *A History of Christianity*, a book that combined his favorite subjects of religion and history.

There were still occasional trips to New York, where Harvie could visit with his son, Lewis, who had accepted a position with Philip Morris after graduating from the University of Virginia. "We both enjoyed good food and good wine and New York City," recalled Lewis. "So when Dad came to town, it was always a treat for me, because we could go to some of the restaurants that he enjoyed, including Giovanni's, and in the evenings we would often have a brandy or two at the King Cole Bar at the St. Regis." In addition, Lewis introduced Harvie to some of the newer, fashionable restaurants in Manhattan. "He took great pride," said Lewis, "in the fact that one time Joe Cullman told him, 'Harvie, I want to take you to dinner at a special place.' And Harvie said, 'What place is that?' And when Joe told him, Harvie said, 'It is a great place, Joe, and Lewis took me there last night.'"

Jay, meanwhile, had obtained his degree from the University of Virginia Law School and had spent a year and a half as a clerk for Lewis Powell, while Powell was sitting as a Justice on the United State Supreme Court. The experience provided Jay with the material for his second book, *Serving Justice: A Supreme Court Clerk's View*, published by Charterhouse Books in 1974. Jay subsequently served as Editor of the Norfolk *Virginian-Pilot*, as a Reagan administration appointee in the Department of Justice, and as a professor at the University of Virginia Law School, before he was appointed in 1984 to the Fourth Circuit Court of Appeals.

For both of his sons, as for many young people at United Virginia Bank and in the community, Harvie served as an advisor and counselor along the paths of their careers. He never insisted that Jay or Lewis follow his footsteps into banking. "Whatever we tried to do," noted Jay, "he tried to support us," though Harvie did complain, with a wink, that he would have been happier if Jay had taken at least one accounting course somewhere along the way.

Harvie and Letitia with Jay and Lossie's children,
James Nelson Wilkinson and Porter Noell Wilkinson.

Harvie and Lewis with Lewis' son John Lewis
Wilkinson.

Just as Harvie had valued so dearly the wisdom of his father, so Jay and Lewis continued to ask Harvie for advice on any difficulties they encountered. "I can hear them now," Letitia recalled with a smile. "When they'd call on the telephone, they'd say, 'Mom, how are you?' and then, barely pausing, 'Is Dad there?'"

Few pleasures of retirement could surpass the delight Harvie took in his grandchildren. First to arrive was James Nelson Wilkinson, who was born in 1977 to Jay and his wife, Lossie. Then, three years later, Jay and Lossie had a daughter, whom they named Porter Noell Wilkinson. Lewis and his wife, Polly, also provided Harvie with a daughterson combination: Mary Elizabeth Barnett, who was also born in 1980, and John Lewis Wilkinson, born in 1989. It was obvious that Harvie cherished his grandchildren immensely; and (according to Jay, at least) allowed them to get away with far more than Jay or Lewis ever could have done.

As proud as he was of his sons and his grandchildren, Harvie always found his greatest joy and solace in the moments he spent alone with Letitia. "It was an extraordinary marriage," said Jay. "She was always the center of his life, and all of his activities and energy came from the support that she gave him." Throughout his years of friendship with Harvie, Lewis Powell always took great pride in the fact that he was the one who had introduced Harvie to Letitia for the first time when they all were young, at the Saturday night dance at Woodberry Forest. "I also claim a major share of credit for your distinguished career," Powell reminded Harvie in a personal note of January 2, 1987, "because, without me, you would not have Letitia!"

Harvie readily acknowledged that he owed everything, including his success in his chosen career, to his wife. "I was never unconscious," he once announced to a gathering of friends, "that my ability to do this competing in a fashion that would give me an inner satisfaction was dependent on Letitia. She was magnificent."

> Those of you who know me intimately are aware of the fact that I move at a very rapid pace. It is not the pace of wisdom. It is the pace of all valves open, and if my sons would ever return to their father's knee and listen with appropriate humility, I would urge them not to go at an all-out, valves-open pace. It is a fool's pace and only an angel can save you. My reserve strength was therefore limited. I never had to call on what was not there because Letitia raised the boys and carried her responsibilities with magnificence and aplomb.

"I was never unconscious that my ability to do this. . .
was dependent on Letitia. She was magnificent."

For their fiftieth wedding anniversary in October 1989, Harvie organized a special gathering of family and friends at Colonial Williamsburg. He chartered a tour bus to take the guests from Richmond to Williamsburg, and then presided over an elegant private dinner at the Williamsburg Inn. At the close of dinner, the assembled friends of Harvie and Letitia offered heartfelt toasts to the many moments of happiness they had enjoyed in their company over the years.

As a measure of the esteem in which his contemporaries held him, and in recognition of his contributions to the educational and financial life of the Commonwealth of Virginia, Harvie was honored by the endowment of a special chair in

Harvie being presented the Darden School Sponsors'
"Distinguished Service Award" in 1983 by Jack Elam III,
President, Darden School Sponsors Trustees.

his name at the Colgate Darden School of Business Administration. In the same spirit, United Virginia Bank made a generous contribution to the Tayloe Murphy Institute at the University of Virginia. In 1983, the Sponsors of the Darden School bestowed the Distinguished Service Award upon Harvie for his numerous contributions to the school. And in May 1989, Harvie Wilkinson, "Virginia's leading banker of his time," was inducted into the Richmond Business Hall of Fame.

In August 1990, while he and Letitia were vacationing at Martha's Vineyard in Massachusetts, Harvie was stricken with a pulmonary illness and severe coughing spells that caused further damage to his already weakened heart. After several days of treatment at a local hospital, his physicians advised that he be moved to a city hospital with more sophisticated cardiovascular equipment. They asked Letitia if she wanted Harvie taken to Boston; with Harvie's approval, she insisted that he be flown to Richmond instead.

A hospital plane brought him back to his native city. Harvie seemed to have survived the trip well, and Letitia was relieved to have him home with Jay and Lewis. That night, in his hospital room, Harvie spoke at length with both his sons. He seemed upbeat, clear-headed, and obviously happy to be home. His sense of humor had returned, as he playfully gave instructions to his nurses. At times he seemed vigorous and full of life, looking forward to the next day, and thinking of the future.

Early the next morning, August 16, 1990, in his beloved Virginia, Harvie Wilkinson suffered a fatal heart attack.

"If ever there was a man who lived his relationship to God, it was most assuredly J. Harvie Wilkinson," affirmed the Reverend Frank F. Fagan, then rector of St. James's Church, which Harvie had served so loyally for nearly 50 years. "Everyone was important to him…his family, his close friends as well as those of even slight acquaintance…people from all walks of life knew his acceptance." □

Harvie gave and gave and gave of his time, talent and treasure. He was a good steward. The generosity he so unselfishly offered to family and friends and institutions was taken by God and blessed. You and I are beneficiaries of this wonderful inheritance from this perfectionist who demanded so much of himself, who unselfishly gave so much of himself, from this man of impatience who wanted things done yesterday but who made you feel you were a VIP and he had lots of time — this man of such respect and great love who was always pointing the way for others. You and I are well challenged to follow his leadership...

— THE REVEREND FRANK F. FAGAN

PHOTOGRAPHY CREDITS

<u>write, restudy, and rewrite</u> until you have evolved a single proposed action — the best one of all you have considered. Your chief should then merely approve or disapprove.

"Do not worry your chief or department head with long explanations and memoranda. <u>Writing a memorandum to your chief does not constitute completed staff work, but writing a memorandum for your chief to send to someone else does.</u> Your views should be placed before him in finished form so that he can make them his views simply by signing his name."

"In most instances, completed staff work results in a single document prepared for the signature of the chief or department head, without accompanying comment. If the proper result is reached, the chief will usually recognize it at once. If he wants a comment or explanation, he will ask for it."

"The practice of completed staff work does not preclude a 'rough draft,' but the rough draft must not be a halfbaked idea. It must be complete in every respect except that it lacks the requisite number of copies and need not be neat. But a rough draft must not be used as an excuse for shifting to the chief the burden of formulating the action."

"The 'completed staff work' theory may result in more work for the staff members, but it results in more freedom for the chief. This is as it should be. Further, it accomplishes two things:

A.   The chief or department head is protected from halfbaked ideas, voluminous memoranda, and immature oral presentations.

B.   The staff member who has a real idea to sell is enabled more readily to find a market.

"When you have finished your 'completed staff work,' the final test is this:

<u>If you were the chief or department head, would you be willing to sign the paper you have prepared, and stake your professional reputation on its being right?</u>

"If the answer is in the negative, take it back and work it over, because it is not yet "completed staff work'."

Harvie engaging in one of the Bank's frequent
motivational sales meetings — "SELL, SELL, SELL!"

All the while, Harvie continued to pound home his theme of "building the
bank." In meeting after meeting, he sought to motivate and encourage State-Planters'
officers and employees to develop new business wherever possible, insisting that they
avail themselves of every opportunity to increase the bank's customer base. It was a task
that Harvie recognized as critical to the future of the bank, for State-Planters was still
imbued in large measure with the gentlemanly atmosphere and unhurried pace of the
prewar banking world. As a team of management consultants observed, "The atmosphere
at the executive level [of State-Planters] is warm, congenial, and 'clubby,'" though sadly
lacking in the sort of "hard-nosed, competitive, imaginative business methods" that
Harvie correctly viewed as essential for survival in a rapidly-changing corporate climate.

"Developing the gross revenue of this bank along all sound lines is our *major*
hope for improved earnings," Harvie informed an officers' meeting in August 1959. "We
have got to learn to be good salesmen in the houses and in the offices of our customers.
The customer calling program is going to be very much revitalized... We hope to have

the whole bank hitting on all fours. In fact we must do it. To repeat, we cannot increase earnings and benefit ourselves except through building the bank."

Again the following month, Harvie urged his staff to accept the premise that selling was an integral part of everyone's duties. "The fact that it is the responsibility and duty *and an important ingredient in the personal advancement* of each of us," he claimed, "has never been burned into our consciousness with a hot branding iron stamped 'SELL, SELL, SELL, SELL.' This must be done. This awareness on the part of every officer and employee is, I believe, essential to produce the type of results we have every reason to think that our talents and our dedication entitle us to achieve."

As part of this strategy (and to improve communications within the bank), Wilkinson inaugurated a series of quarterly meetings of all officers of State-Planters. Usually these gatherings were held at the Commonwealth Club in Richmond, where the bank executives (about fifty gentlemen) would gather first for a cocktail hour, followed by dinner and wine, and a speech by Harvie. For Harvie, these get-togethers were a welcome opportunity "to crook an elbow, break bread, sass one another, and exchange serious ideas." His speeches might center around specific suggestions for the bank, as when he urged his colleagues in July 1963 to focus on moderate-sized corporate clients, because "this is our natural market. This is our market indigenous to the Richmond area. This is our market where [personal] interplay between us and our customer can be best activated and kept in motion."

On another occasion, Harvie suggested that "if we *think* better lending, better investments, better trusts, better auditing, and better bookkeeping and *do* better lending, better investments, better trust work, better auditing, and better bookkeeping, we will have better personalities in our bank, because this excellence of performance flowing from the right mental attitude of attack and conquering will be reflected in our own individual personalities in giving to us a sense of accomplishment, a sense of achievement, that in turn will be reflected in our manner and bearing to the customers."

Or Harvie might allow himself a broader look at the world of banking and finance. At the officers' meeting of September 1959, for instance, Harvie suggested that, "contrary to what history records, the banking business is to an increasing degree today becoming a fast moving business. It is no longer the static business of history. Look at the evolution of consumer credit... Remind yourself of the use of computers. Look at the number of branches. Banking, I submit, is moving fast and not enough of our people have moved equally fast in the mental shift."

Although Harvie's messages invariably were delivered with eloquence and wit, a portion of his audience would occasionally be lost in a post-prandial haze, and hence found it difficult to keep up with his train of thought, while others (as one participant put it) were "somewhat less interested" in discussions of the bank's internal operations or weighty matters of economics "than they might have been at another time of day, or under different circumstances."

In his role as the chief executive of State-Planters, Wilkinson readily accepted an obligation to maintain the high degree of visibility in the corporate community that he had already displayed. In September 1959, for instance, he accepted election as a member of the board of the directors of the Freeport Sulphur Company. The following month, he was named to the board of the Life Insurance Company of Virginia.

Even more important was the work that remained to be done in attracting desirable industries to Virginia. Just as he urged his colleagues at State-Planters to dedicate themselves to "building the bank," so Wilkinson spread the gospel of economic growth and modernization throughout the state. "For Virginia to accomplish what her people will expect and demand," he wrote in an open letter to the editor of the *Roanoke Times,* "she must have a fruitful, burgeoning economy... This economy must be strengthened and broadened if the people of Virginia are to have opportunities to earn incomes comparable to those of people in other states, and if the revenues needed by the state are to be forthcoming without a crushing burden on existing businesses and people."

Specifically, Harvie wished to encourage manufacturing concerns to locate their operations in Virginia:

> Let it not be forgotten that manufacturing is the most generative of the various forms of economic activity. Increases in manufacturing are essential if our people moving off the farms are to find employment in manufacturing and those service businesses which are induced to start up by the presence of industry.

Apparently the General Assembly received the message loud and clear, for in 1960 the state legislature established the Virginia Industrial Development Corporation.

The purpose of the VIDC was to extend loans to those businesses that were unable to obtain financing through the normal channels of commercial banks. Similar agencies were already in existence in seventeen other states, and the *Richmond Times-Dispatch* predicted that the VIDC would "fill a long-felt need in Virginia, which has been at a disadvantage in competing with such neighboring states as North and South Carolina." Not surprisingly, Harvie Wilkinson was one of the five members of the VIDC executive board at its inception; his presence was widely regarded as a guarantee of the soundness of the venture.

Shortly after the formation of the VIDC, Wilkinson accepted an opportunity to contribute to the cause of public education, always so dear to his heart. Besides, Harvie recognized that a sound system of public education — and a satisfying quality of life overall — would help entice corporations to move to Richmond and Virginia. "What industry seeks," he informed the Finance Committee of the General Assembly in February 1960, "is a state in which the tax structure is fairly balanced *and a state in which the Governmental services of schools and roads and recreation and the other facets of living are not merely adequate but are attractive* in comparison with those provided by competing states." [italics added]

In April 1961, the Richmond City Council unanimously voted to ask Harvie to fill a vacancy on the city's school board, replacing his old friend Lewis F. Powell, Jr., who had recently been appointed to the State Board of Education. The selection certainly pleased the editors of the *Times-Dispatch*, who wrote that "it is fortunate indeed for Richmond that a citizen with Harvie Wilkinson's scholarly mind, sound business sense and broad civic concern is willing to devote his time and thought to the welfare of the city's public school system."

Since Harvie did not claim to be an instant expert in the affairs of the Richmond school system, he took the time to personally visit each public school in the city in the company of the school superintendent. There was certainly no doubt that Harvie possessed definite ideas about the direction education should take in the 1960s. He strongly supported increased school construction and higher salaries for teachers, to allow the city — and, for that matter, the entire state, which ranked 37th among the 50 states in pay for high school teachers — to compete with the rest of the nation for the best educators. To help reform the state-county relationship in education, Harvie further

The newest member of the Richmond School Board,
April, 1961.

suggested that the state donate a basic sum to the counties for their schools, while
requiring the counties to meet certain standards of excellence to remain eligible for
future state grants. All the while, Harvie remained cognizant of the need to avoid
overburdening individuals and states with excessive taxes. And this brought him back
once again to his theme of economic expansion, to the fundamental requirement to
"grow the economy" of Virginia so educational appropriations could be increased without
undue hardship on the existing tax base.

Along with his economic and educational reform recommendations, Harvie also
urged the state government to examine its own administrative structure, to determine
what functions might be handled more efficiently, "with a view to attaining desired goals
through doing things differently from the way we have been doing them." Clearly he
understood that this would not be easy for such a conservative society as Virginia's, "for it
tears at roots." Nevertheless, he deemed it essential if the state were not to be over-
whelmed by financial costs.

Harvie (far right) and his colleagues on the Commission
to Study State Government discuss their plans with
Governor Almond, September 1961.

Wilkinson soon had the chance to translate his suggestions into reality when he
was named vice chairman of the Governor's Commission to Study the State Government
in 1960-61. After more than a year's study, the Commission delivered its report to
Governor J. Lindsay Almond, Jr. on September 23, 1961. Its most significant proposal
was the establishment of a new Department of Economic Development to augment and
coordinate the state's efforts to compete for industry. Prior to this time, there was no
effective statewide agency of industrial development in Virginia; such activity as existed
had been submerged in the Department of Conservation and Planning, where a few
employees engaged in a desultory effort to attract new business to the Commonwealth.
For the past few years, a coalition of Virginia business and civic leaders — including
Harvie Wilkinson, of course — had been lobbying for the establishment of a separate
organization devoted solely to the cause of economic development, and their efforts
finally paid fruit with the Governor's acceptance of the Commission's report.

In addition to the formation of the Department of Economic Development, the Commission recommended increased staffing for the Governor's Office to permit it to engage more effectively in long-range planning and direction of state programs; professionalization of the State Council of Higher Education; consolidation and simplification of the administrative structure of the state Department of Education; and the reestablishment of a Department of Conservation to deal with the state's forestry, mineral resources, water, and parks.

As visible as Wilkinson was in civic affairs during these years, perhaps his most valuable contribution to the welfare of the state occurred out of the public view. Ever since the United States Supreme Court declared segregated public schools unconstitutional in its landmark decision of *Brown vs. Board of Education* in 1954, public school systems throughout the South had been struggling to find some means to avoid integration and its perceived social and educational consequences. In Virginia, where the state constitution expressly stated that "white and colored children shall not be taught in the same school," the battle against enforcement of the Court's decree was led by the slowly weakening but still-powerful old-line political organization of Senator Harry Flood Byrd, Sr. At first the opposition sought to evade compliance with the Court's decision through legal methods, but as efforts for compromise appeared doomed to failure, segregationist sentiment began to harden.

"If we can organize the Southern States for massive resistance to this order," proclaimed Senator Byrd in February 1956, "I think that in time the rest of the country will realize that racial integration is not going to be accepted in the South." Almost immediately, the term "massive resistance" became the battle cry of the arch-conservative opposition to integration. As one perceptive observer of the ensuing political crisis has pointed out, "Massive resistance was also the last triumphant gesture of the old order of Virginia politics — a twilight performance where the hard-core coalition of the old Byrd organization raised its last great hosannas."

In a special session in late 1956, the General Assembly voted to cut off funds to any local school district willing to open its schools on an integrated basis. Two years later, in the fall of 1958, Governor Almond dutifully closed all high schools in the cities of Charlottesville and Norfolk, as well as those in Warren and Prince Edward counties. Although some students enrolled in hastily-organized private schools, others lost an

Governor Almond making an emphatic point during
the "massive resistance" controversy.

entire year of schooling. The resulting chaos caused considerable distress to Harvie
Wilkinson, Lewis F. Powell, Jr., and a score of prominent Virginia business and professional leaders, who realized that the ongoing massive resistance controversy was doing
irreparable harm to the Commonwealth.

Although Harvie Wilkinson had usually supported the Byrd organization in the
past, and certainly did not consider himself a liberal on the subject of integration, he
recognized clearly the moral and economic implications of this issue. As Jay Wilkinson
later recalled, Harvie "was very emphatic on the need to end massive resistance. He
thought, first of all, that it just wasn't right, as a matter of legal defiance and moral
posture. And second of all, he thought it was hurting educational opportunity badly,
that it was giving Virginia a bad name nationwide, and that it was going to discourage
businesses from locating here, and would stunt economic opportunity for the people
of the state."

Following a particularly fiery speech of defiance in early November 1958, Governor Almond received an invitation from a group of twenty-nine of the state's leading business executives (including Harvie Wilkinson) to meet with them at the Rotunda Club in Richmond. At the ensuing dinner conference, Wilkinson and his colleagues informed the governor that, in their opinion, massive resistance was doomed to failure, would certainly produce "untold harm" to the Commonwealth, and was bound to adversely affect Virginia's economy and image. Although Almond responded with a stinging rebuke to the businessmen and a pledge never to accept integration, within a few days he had begun to moderate his position.

The following month, both the Virginia Supreme Court of Appeals and a federal district court in Norfolk declared the state's school-closing statutes illegal. Although die-hard opponents of integration abandoned the fight only gradually and grudgingly, the immediate crisis had passed, and the forces of moderation and economic progressivism had merged victorious and even strengthened by the struggle. It was now time for Harvie Wilkinson to turn his attention to another challenge: the creation of an entirely novel form of financial organization in Virginia, suitable to the needs of the state in the last half of the twentieth century — a bank holding company that would become known as United Virginia Bankshares. □

IV

THE DREAM FULFILLED

*I was utterly and totally sensitive to this
inability to bring ourselves to birth — in the
sense of being born in the 20th century —
because we lacked the economic muscle.*

— J. HARVIE WILKINSON, JR.

$\mathbf{E}$arly in 1961, State-Planters faced its first significant credit crisis since the 1920s. Essentially, the bank found itself without enough deposits to make all the loans it wanted to make. Certainly State-Planters was not alone in this predicament, for the United States economy in the early 1960s was on the verge of another prolonged period of expansion, and the nationwide demand for credit already had begun to far outpace the supply of money.

It had long been an axiom of commercial banking that a bank's customers would never simultaneously request to use their full lines of credit, any more than its depositors would all ask to withdraw their money at the same time. But as an increasing number of State-Planters' corporate customers started to borrow significant amounts of funds, Harvie Wilkinson and his colleagues grew seriously concerned about the bank's ability to meet its commitments. Yet State-Planters clearly did not want to set a precedent by turning down any customer's request for funds; if the bank had suggested that a corporation look elsewhere for credit, it probably would have lost that customer forever. "So for the first time," recalled Dick Dilworth, "we literally began to almost ration credit.

We were told to dampen our efforts, to stop trying to drum up new loan business, which was just contrary to the way things had been." To explain his proposed strategy to the bank's officers, Harvie went so far as to issue a memorandum entitled (in quintessentially Wilkinsonian style) "The Coordination of the Effectuation of our Loan Policy."

Although the emergency passed without causing undue hardship to State-Planters, it served as another vivid reminder that the largest Virginia banks were in serious danger of falling far behind their counterparts in other states due to their inability to meet the credit and service demands of corporations and a rapidly growing population. Despite the mergers that leading Richmond banks such as State-Planters and First and Merchants had effected in the late 1950s, the Commonwealth's banking resources remained dangerously fragmented; so "fractionalized," in Harvie Wilkinson's words, that Virginia ranked 43rd out of 50 states in the percentage of total bank resources that were held by each state's 10 largest banks.

Indeed, every adjacent state except West Virginia — and every South Atlantic state except South Carolina — boasted at least one bank with greater assets than any financial institution in Virginia, and the disparity was steadily increasing. "Virginia," Harvie lamented, "is almost surrounded by states in which there are large banking complexes which are competing with the much smaller Virginia banks for the business of large national and regional corporations."

Virginia banks were even starting to lose business to competitors in Philadelphia and New York. "I think a lot of pressure came from what Harvie saw happening around us in the neighboring states, particularly to the South," noted Lewis Flinn, a State-Planters official who had joined the bank upon graduating from the University of Virginia Graduate School of Business Administration in 1957. "North Carolina had statewide branching, and the banks were getting much bigger. And here we were, losing our relative size by our inability to expand and grow like a lot of banks could in other states. That type of pressure was building very rapidly." Paul Sackett, then the chief executive officer of First National Trust and Savings Bank in Lynchburg, agreed with Flinn's assessment. "That was what had Harvie and his colleagues so upset," said Sackett. "They thought that it was a disservice to the state of Virginia for this condition to exist."

For several years, Harvie Wilkinson had been holding informal discussions with other leading Virginia bankers to examine various alternatives for expanding the capabilities of the Commonwealth's banking system. Specifically, of course, Harvie was searching for the best means to expand the resources of State-Planters. Now, in the spring of 1961, Harvie decided that the time for action had arrived. At the time, there was really only one avenue available, a relatively recent option that had been opened in 1956 through the passage of federal legislation permitting banks to establish holding companies under certain restrictive conditions.

Prior to that time, Congress had consistently extolled the virtues of a decentralized American banking system characterized by hundreds of small banks operating independently in local communities across the nation. This policy had been born of the fear of panics instilled by the financial crises of 1906 and 1931-32, when large segments of the United States banking system appeared to be in imminent danger of collapse. The federal government subsequently sought stability in the diffusion of capital resources and the sheer number of banks; by 1960, for instance, there were 13,999 commercial banks in existence in the U.S. Further, Congress accepted the premise that local investors and bank officials would possess detailed knowledge of their own markets, and thus would be less likely to make excessively risky loans.

By the mid-1950s, however, there was a growing sense within Congress and the financial community that the nation's banking laws were archaic, and that the restrictions of the National Banking Act and the Glass-Steagall Act had outlived their usefulness. Hence Congress enacted the Registered Bank Holding Company Act of 1956, which permitted the formation of bank holding companies, albeit under severe limitations. For instance, a bank holding company could not own any business other than a bank; nor could a holding company own a bank outside the state in which the holding company's lead bank was located. "So what was being created from 1956 through the 1960s," explained one expert, "was a number of bank holding companies that were using this device to spread out *within* their own state."

For Harvie Wilkinson, the concept of a bank holding company seemed almost ideally suited both to his goals for the expansion of State-Planters, and to the unique circumstances of the Virginia banking community, for the holding company structure permitted individual banks to come together under a single corporate umbrella while retaining a significant degree of autonomy in their day-to-day operations. As Wilkinson himself later pointed out,

The major advantage of a bank holding company, to the surprise of some people, related not solely to economics but rather to psychology. The people of Virginia are not the first to try something new. They are inclined to a more measured pace... It was clear to me that the psychology for affiliation among the Virginia banks was going to require a period of confederation — a period of getting to know each other before we could ultimately move to what [later became known as] the 'single bank' holding company.

Wilkinson was not the first Virginia banker to discern the benefits of a statewide bank holding company. For some time, bankers and business executives across the Commonwealth had been discussing the advantages of such an entity as a means of meeting the anticipated demand for more substantial and sophisticated financial services. In fact, the Bank of Virginia, under the leadership of Thomas Boushall, had previously stolen a march on the rest of the banking community by establishing branches through-out the state in the late 1940s.

At that time, banks could establish branches in any city of over 25,000 people in Virginia. But the success of the Bank of Virginia's expansion campaign had alarmed Boushall's more cautious competitors, who succeeded in persuading the Virginia General Assembly to pass restrictive legislation in 1948 prohibiting any bank from establishing branches outside the city where its main office was located. At the same time, mergers between banks were limited to institutions in the same or contiguous counties. Since the General Assembly could hardly undo what Boushall already had wrought, however, the net effect of the legislation was to maintain the Bank of Virginia's position as the only bank with statewide connections. The only consolation for the rest of the financial community was the fact that the Bank of Virginia was not a full-fledged commercial bank, but a Morris Plan institution whose primary focus was on providing services to individual consumers.

Even though Harvie Wilkinson and other forward-looking members of the Virginia banking community recognized that the time had arrived to ease the restrictions on statewide banking in Virginia, the balance of power still appeared to reside with the small, country banks that resisted any attempt by their urban counterparts to intrude

Lewis F. Powell, Jr., member of the Board of Directors,
State-Planters Bank of Commerce and Trusts, 1959-1963
and Director, United Virginia Bankshares, 1963-1971.

upon their markets. The extent of their opposition to any change in the Commonwealth's banking laws was graphically illustrated in June 1961, at the annual convention of the Virginia Bankers Association, when a coalition of small banks fought back a proposal (known as the Virginia Metropolitan Plan) that would have permitted statewide mergers between banks with head offices located in major urban areas.

Undaunted, Wilkinson — accompanied by State-Planters' counsel, Lewis F. Powell, Jr. — embarked in the summer of 1961 upon a month-long tour across the Commonwealth. At each stop, Wilkinson and Powell met with the senior members of key committees of the General Assembly, explaining in detail the debilitating effects of the existing banking restrictions upon the economic development of Virginia. "If a state is to develop and maintain a vigorous industrial economy," Harvie warned at one point, "it must develop and maintain a vigorous banking system with units of a size sufficient to accommodate the growing financing needs of the commerce and industry their services foster." "Harvie by this time had become a very influential citizen of the state," remarked Powell. "He was very persuasive, and I was his back-up man."

Meanwhile, the defeat of the Metropolitan Plan had confirmed Wilkinson in his decision to expand State-Planters via the holding company route. As a preliminary step, Harvie dispatched a team of bank officers on a fact-finding tour to study several bank holding companies that were already in existence, notably Northwest Bancorp and First Bankstock Corporation in Minneapolis — both of which had been formed in the 1930s to help rescue troubled banks in that region — and Marine Midland in Buffalo, New York.

The reports from Minneapolis and Buffalo provided further evidence that the bank holding company structure was well-suited to State-Planters' needs. Beyond the psychological advantages Wilkinson had noted, the holding company would allow State-Planters to expand more fully throughout the state, since merged banks were still prohibited by law from branching into any areas outside their home offices. Although Harvie realized from the outset that a holding company was a looser form of organization than a single, closely united bank system, and would require time, persistence, and patience to tighten the administrative structure of a holding company, he was willing to pay that price.

Once the means of expansion for State-Planters had been determined, the next task was to target specific markets for expansion and initiate negotiations with the leading banks in those areas, to assess their willingness to participate in the venture. For Wilkinson, the considerations that would govern the choice of markets seemed clear from the outset. "The primary considerations," he explained, "were geography and population."

> We wanted to be in the dynamic areas, the faster growing areas of the Commonwealth. That meant getting into Northern Virginia and the peninsula of Virginia, and eventually into Norfolk.

> We also wanted to have broad, geographic diversification through-out the state so that if one area had a depressed economy, the diminished earning power of that bank could hopefully be offset by the better earning power of other banks in other economic areas of the state that did not have the dominant segment of their economy in depression.

Accordingly, Wilkinson and his colleagues decided to focus their efforts upon obtaining representation for the holding company in the rapidly-growing Northern Virginia area, in western Virginia — notably in Charlottesville, Lynchburg, and Roanoke — and the Tidewater region, particularly in the urban centers of Norfolk and Newport News. As he planned his strategy, Harvie would often unfurl a map of Virginia, spreading it across a desk and placing pennies on every city where he wanted the holding company to go. (Lewis Powell kept suggesting that he use dimes instead, but Harvie insisted that he could see those pennies better; besides, he could more readily afford them.)

From the start, Wilkinson found a willing ally in Clarence J. Robinson, the president of First and Citizens National Bank in Alexandria. Robinson was a gentle, courtly man whose experience as an industrialist had earned him a reputation as one of Northern Virginia's leading corporate citizens. Since the late 1940s, he and Harvie had served together on the Board of Trustees of the Church Schools in the Diocese of Virginia; together, they had helped rescue the schools from a staggering burden of debt by restructuring and rationalizing the Church Schools' finances. For the past several years, Robinson and Wilkinson had been discussing, albeit in a desultory manner, the possibility of some sort of union between their banks. By 1961, Robinson had become convinced that decisive action was imperative, due to the increasing competition he was facing from Financial General Corporation, a Washington, D.C., conglomerate holding company with diverse investments in banks, insurance, and industrial enterprises, and First Virginia Corporation (now First Virginia Banks, Inc.), based in Arlington.

Clarence Robinson's easy-going manner (Harvie affectionately referred to him as "Ol' Blue Eyes") disguised a first-rate executive temperament; as Paul Sackett noted, "Clarence didn't have any problem making decisions." Robinson did, however, occasionally express a certain measure of bewilderment at the erudite language habitually employed by his good friend from Richmond. Robinson claimed,

> To analyze Harvie's prose, you first had the three and four syllable words, such as 'proliferation,' 'fractionalization,' and then 'fluidity' — you could feel it drift. All of them mixed with a little French to give verve and a little Latin for erudition and a wee touch of Greek used sparingly and seldom for surprise and bafflement.

Clarence D. Robinson, "Ol' Blue Eyes," President of First and Citizens National Bank of Alexandria.

On occasions when English, Latin, French and Greek failed, Harvie could just as easily as rolling off a log come up with words seldom used such as "doable." Oh, how we loved "doable." Whether it was a merger, or whatever it might be, "doable" came into the picture...

I remember my first encounter with *de novo*. I didn't know what the hell *de novo* meant. I knew it wasn't a word that had to do with warehousing, and I was too proud to ask what it meant, so I said I'm just going to sit around and let *de novo* expose itself. So I watched and waited. We talked of growing by merger, by branching, and then by *de novo*. But we never did the word — *de novoed*! Finally, I came to the conclusion that it was a little known section of Fredericksburg — a Garden of Eden — a place to retire to where all is calm and serene.

In any event, Robinson informed Harvie that he was prepared to commit his bank to a holding company if Wilkinson and State-Planters would take the lead in forming the new venture. Harvie agreed, and he and Burwell Gunn (who headed up State-Planters' trust department) traveled up to Alexandria to work out the details in a series of meetings at Robinson's home. According to Wilkinson, the enthusiastic participation of First and Citizens lent a powerful impetus to the venture, "because it showed that this wish [for a bank holding company] had its genesis other than in Richmond."

Robinson then joined Wilkinson and Gunn in a journey to Lynchburg and Roanoke, to try to persuade the leaders of the largest banks in each of those cities to become a part of their endeavor. They found Paul Sackett quite receptive. "They came by here in the morning," Sackett recalled laconically, "and stopped and chatted with me for a little while." Sackett, too, had discussed the matter previously with Wilkinson. "This was not altogether new to me," he noted, "and I was interested in what they said."

Briefly, Wilkinson and Robinson pointed out the benefits that would accrue from a statewide banking organization — primarily the enhanced capabilities for providing loans and services — and particularly the advantages of the holding company structure. "Harvie said, 'You could do two things,'" remembered Sackett. "'One, we will get the better people to come with us if we tell them that they're going to run their own show and have their own independent operation. And furthermore, you could branch from each one of those individual banks that you had in your holding company.'"

While Wilkinson, Robinson, and Gunn continued on to Roanoke to hold a similar conversation with the president of First National Exchange Bank (later Dominion Bankshares), Sackett telephoned several of his directors and discussed the proposal with them. "They said, 'Sure, forge ahead,'" said Sackett. "And so we did." Sackett gave Harvie and his colleagues the good news — subject to approval by First National's stockholders — on their way back through Lynchburg. Undoubtedly Wilkinson and Robinson were glad to receive it, since the president of the Roanoke bank had rejected their overture, partly because of sectional pride (he had no intention of joining a confederation headed by a Richmond bank), and partly because he was already planning to form a separate bank holding company.

Over the next few months, Wilkinson and Robinson succeeded in attracting three more banks to their consortium. Each of these institutions shared Wilkinson's concern that the fractionalization of banking resources was adversely affecting their ability to supply the quality and scope of banking services that their communities required. The addition of Citizens Marine Jefferson Bank in Newport News gave the holding company a presence in the Tidewater, with its heavy concentration of defense and shipbuilding industries. A second Northern Virginia bank, the Vienna Trust Company, provided access to the rapidly-expanding Washington, D.C. suburban communities of McLean, Great Falls, and Tysons Corner. The final member of the original group was the Merchants and Farmers Bank of Franklin. Although the Franklin Bank, located in southside Virginia, was somewhat smaller than the others, it brought into the holding company Merchant and Farmers' principal stockholder, Colgate W. Darden, Jr., the former Governor of the Commonwealth who had recently retired as President of the University of Virginia.

Together, the consortium controlled assets totalling more than $350 million. It would be impossible to overestimate the role that personal relationships between the presidents of these six banks played in bringing together this remarkable aggregation of financial resources and executive talent. Although they understood that they would retain a significant degree of autonomy under the holding company structure, it still required a substantial measure of trust for them to leave the comfort of traditional custom and embark on a voyage that would lead their institutions into uncharted waters, especially since State-Planters was by far the largest bank in the original group, with more than three and a half times the assets of the next largest bank. Probably the deciding factor, for most, was Harvie Wilkinson's pledge that the holding company would be organized along the lines of participatory democracy. As Lewis Flinn, the first secretary of the holding company, later pointed out, "I think there was a lot of genuine respect within the presidencies of the group for Harvie and the others here at State-Planters."

The result of all these negotiations would have been considerably less effective if the General Assembly had not rescinded its ban on statewide banking. Shortly after the legislature convened on January 10, 1962, a measure to liberalize Virginia's banking laws was introduced in both houses. Known as the Buck-Holland bill, it included provisions to permit statewide mergers between banks that had been in operation for at least five years, and to allow branching in cities contiguous to the city or county in which the parent bank was located. Branching from any bank acquired by merger, however, was still

Paul E. Sackett, President of First National Trust and Savings Bank, and a leading member of the Lynchburg business community.

prohibited. Although the Buck-Holland measure generated considerable controversy, the groundwork laid by Wilkinson and Powell over the previous summer paved the way for its eventual approval by the Assembly, and on July 1, 1962, Governor Albertis Harrison signed the bill into law.

For a brief moment, Harvie pondered anew the relative merits of expanding via a holding company, or through mergers according to the terms of the Buck-Holland bill. But only for a moment. Then the presidents of the six banks entered into a final series of negotiations to bring the holding company into existence.

Since the banks were forming a new corporation, they needed to devise a fair and reasonable formula to transfer the existing shares of their banks into shares of the holding company. A difficulty arose in deciding the ratio to be used, based upon the comparative value of each bank's stock. That is, someone had to determine what factors should be taken into account (present assets, past profits, potential for future growth), and the relative weight each of those factors should receive. There were, in effect, almost limitless variations on this theme, and it is not surprising that the banks finally approved Wilkinson's recommendation that they invite an expert, impartial third party — the investment firm of First Boston Corporation — to solve this thorny problem.

After several months of study, First Boston unveiled its recommendations to the bank executives — and Harvie Wilkinson nearly fainted from the shock. He had expected that State-Planters, as the largest and best-earning bank in the consortium, might have to make concessions to its new partners, but the formula that First Boston had devised seemed to have significantly undervalued State-Planters' stock. What had happened was that First Boston had given substantially greater weight to the banks' potential for future growth, while discounting their past and present performance. This had the effect of increasing the value of the shares of the Northern Virginia banks, since the Washington suburbs were expanding more rapidly than the Richmond or Shenandoah regions.

In any event, a shocked Harvie Wilkinson indicated that the proposed formula would never obtain the approval of the State-Planters shareholders. At that point, Clarence Robinson and Paul Sackett asked Harvie to join them for a brief private conference. "They went out into a little anteroom," recalled Dick Dilworth, "while everyone else stood around and bit their fingernails, wondering if this whole thing, these several years of trying to put this holding company together, was all going to blow up because of this."

But they had come too far to permit the project to be derailed at the final moment. Over the next fifteen minutes, Wilkinson, Robinson, and Sackett determined what adjustments would be needed to make the formula more equitable. Together, they worked out a statesmanlike compromise that allowed the holding company to move forward. Although there was further minor tinkering with the formula (and some last-minute personal diplomacy by Harvie) to satisfy one of the smaller banks in the consortium, the transfer of shares proceeded smoothly.

As the architect of the holding company, Harvie Wilkinson was the natural choice to be elected its first president and chief executive officer. Clarence Robinson was elected chairman of the board of directors, and Paul Sackett agreed to serve as chairman of the executive committee. Each of the six bank presidents was named to the holding company's board of directors, along with a small number of other senior executives from each member of the consortium. From the start, Harvie made a special effort to attract leading members of the Virginia financial and industrial community to the board, to provide the holding company with the best advice available. The original board, for instance, included such prominent individuals as Lewis F. Powell, Jr.; Carlisle Humelsine, the president of Colonial Williamsburg, Inc.; Webster Rhoads, chairman of Miller & Rhoads; Lloyd Noland, chairman of the Newport News-based Noland Company, Inc.; and Sture Olsson, president of the Chesapeake Corporation of Virginia in West Point, Virginia.

There remained only the approval of the Board of Governors of the Federal Reserve System. This was no small matter, considering the relative size of the proposed holding company — it would clearly become the largest aggregation of banking resources in Virginia — and the heretofore fragmented nature of the Commonwealth's banking environment. To obtain the Board's consent, Wilkinson and his associates needed to demonstrate the benefits that would accrue from the establishment of the holding company, while assuaging the Board's concerns that it would significantly hinder competition.

They also needed a name for the holding company. In all the planning meetings that had been held over the previous eighteen months, the banks had never been able to agree on a name. Harvie realized that the other five affiliates would never agree to a name that included either "State" or "Planters," but he insisted upon an explicit recognition of the holding company's unique character and environment. According to Robert Buford, an attorney with Hunton & Williams who helped draft the holding company's charter, the decision on a name came down to the final moments before the charter was actually filed. "I called Harvie," recalled Buford, "and I said, 'Harvie, I've got to have a name in there. I can't file the charter with a blank.' And he said, 'Well, what are you going to do?' I said, 'Well, it's going to be a unit*ed* bank, because it's going to unite six banks. It's going to be a *Virginia* bank [holding company]. And you can't use the word 'bank,' because state law prohibits it. So let's call it *bankshares*, and then we'll say *incorporated*.'" And so the proposed holding company officially became known as United Virginia Bankshares Incorporated.

On July 9, 1962, United Virginia Bankshares Incorporated filed an application with the Board of Governors of the Federal Reserve System to obtain approval to become a bank holding company under the terms of the federal Bank Holding Company Act of

1956. The application made clear the reasons why the formation of the holding company was critical for the future of the Virginia economy: first, "to promote the economic development" of the communities present served by the individual banks; second, "to develop a banking system which, because of its size and the location of its Subsidiary Banks, can supply the need for increased and expanded banking services in Virginia"; and third, to enable UVB "to compete more effectively with banking institutions located in neighboring states which are much larger than any of the Subsidiary Banks."

To obtain approval, however, the application needed to convince the Board of Governors that the formation of UVB would not have a significantly deleterious effect upon other banks in Virginia, or create a holding company so large that it would adversely impact the public interest. Despite the fact that UVB would control only slightly more than 10 percent of the total banking resources in the Commonwealth, the issue of competition temporarily became a sticking point when counsel for the Department of Justice objected to the application in November 1962, largely on the grounds that the holding company purportedly would dominate banking in Northern Virginia. (The Department's opposition did not come as any surprise, since it had opposed virtually every other proposed bank merger and holding company of any consequence in the United States in recent years.)

Fortunately for the future of Virginia, the Board of Governors took a broader view of the issue. Dismissing the Justice Department's concerns as unwarranted, the Board pointed out that even after the formation of the holding company, six of the state's ten largest banks would remain independent. It also noted that both the Virginia State Corporation Commission and the Comptroller of the Currency had strongly endorsed the venture. Accordingly, the Board of Governors — in a narrow 4-3 decision — approved United Virginia Bankshares' application on December 6, and on January 10, 1963, United Virginia Bankshares began operations at its offices at Ninth and Main Streets in Richmond.

At the outset, United Virginia Bankshares had — through its six affiliate banks — 45 offices serving eleven cities and counties, and $454 million in assets. Yet initially, the holding company itself possessed only four full-time employees: Senior vice president Moncure Patteson, who handled the day-to-day operations of the holding company; corporate secretary and treasurer Lewis Flinn; a bookkeeper, and a secretary.

Biggest Va. Holding Firm Set

The Federal Reserve Board in Washington has authorized the creation of the largest bank holding company in Virginia.

The board yesterday authorized United Virginia Bankshares Inc. of Richmond to acquire controlling in-

Roanoke Times

VOL. 12, NO. 121 **Saturday**

Bank Mergers and the Economy

A pattern is beginning to form in bank mergers and formation of bank holding companies in Virginia. Although bank holding company legislation has been on the books for years in Virginia, the activity in banking circles in recent months was actually sparked by the merger legislation approved by the last General Assembly.

Latest development is the announcement of plans for formation of United Virginia Bankshares, Inc., a holding company which would be composed of six Virginia banks with $416.6 million in total resources. It would be the biggest bank holding company in the state.

One bank holding company, First Virginia Corp., already is operating in the state and another, Virginia

still other mergers and perhaps still a ing company prope

In essence, wha is providing the sc proved banking could aid immedi state's industrial a proposed new banking resource loans to a single as an industrial to build a big Such borrowers single institution eral, in negotiati

Virginia has industrial relatio tainly one of of promotion dustry is assets ample assist

shington P

RIDAY, DECEMBER 7, 1962

Capital Commerce

Fed Approves New Bank Chain in Va.

By S. Oliver Goodman
Financial Editor

The Federal Reserve Board has approved the formation of United Virginia Bankshares Corp., a new holding company which will own majority interest in six Virginia banks with resources of more than $397 million.

...ation was by a 6-1

The acquisition of more than 50 per cent of the outstanding stock the six banks, a spokesman said, ill give newly-formed United irginia Bankshares majority ownrship of institutions representing 0.4 per cent of the total resources of all Virginia banks as of June 30, 1962.

Resources of the four other participating banks in United Virginia as of June 30 were First National Trust & Savings Bank, Lynchburg, $37.8 million; Citizens Marine Jefferson Bank, Newport News, $20.5 million; Vienna Trust Co., Vienna, $16.9 million, and Merchants & Farmers Bank, Franklin, $5.7 million.

Two other bank holding companies have heretofore been approved in Virginia by the Federal Reserve Board under the Federal Bank Holding Company Act of

hington S

ON, D.C., FRIDAY, DECEMBER 7, 1962

Virginia Bank Holding Firm Wins Approval

The Federal Reserve Board has approved formation of Ur Virginia Bankshares, Inc., the bank holding company in which and Citizens National Bank of Alexandria and the Vienna Co., of Vienna, Va., are participating, it was announced yest Other Virginia banks participating include: The State-Pl

Six-Bank System Approved

Holding Firm Largest in State

By Larry Weekley
T-D Business Editor

Six Virginia banks including
State-Planters of R

United Virginia Bankshares wins approval from the Federal Reserve Board, December 6, 1962.

The culmination of years of hard work and dedication:
Harvie celebrates the official birth of United Virginia
Bankshares.

As Harvie and Clarence Robinson had promised, there was no attempt to interfere with
the autonomy of the affiliate banks in their communities. Rather, UVB concentrated
upon searching for ways in which it could use the expertise and experience of one or
more of its members to help the others, or pool its resources to increase the efficiency of
common operations. In short, the concept of the holding company in the beginning was
more of an investor than a manager. "They didn't have too much to supervise us with,"
noted Paul Sackett. "It wasn't set up that way. We got more advice than anything else,
and it was a question of how much of it you took."

In the area of bond portfolio management, for instance, most of the affiliate
banks drew upon the expertise of State-Planters' investment department — much as
State-Planters' correspondent banks had done for years — until the holding company
hired its own investment officer, a transplanted Texan named Thomas H. Flinn, in
1964. In the same year, United Virginia Bankshares established its own industrial development office as well. Accounting procedures were gradually standardized, a regional

advertising program was launched, and UVB began to coordinate its affiliate banks' marketing programs.

Perhaps the most significant advance lay in the creation of a large-scale pool for capital lending. In 1963, the combined lending limits of the affiliate banks was over $4.7 million, though the holding company structure made the process of extending credit somewhat awkward. Each bank still made its own loan decisions, which meant that whenever UVB wanted to extend the maximum credit line to a corporate customer, it needed to obtain approval from each of the six banks.

Wilkinson, of course, had recognized from the start that the holding company structure was a loose form of organization that would not immediately provide United Virginia Bankshares with what he termed "the compact thrust that comes from a closely united branch system." While Harvie looked forward to the day when UVB *would* enjoy the sort of compact thrust that would permit it to perform to its maximum efficiency — "to render the best possible service to the people you serve at the best possible profit to the shareholders who are the owners of the bank" — he also understood that the process of tightening the UVB administrative structure would be an evolutionary one.

Meanwhile, the holding company structure *did* facilitate the vital process of expansion. In the early years, the subject of expansion tended to dominate the monthly meetings of the UVB Executive Committee, which initially consisted of the six bank presidents. There were disagreements from time to time, but Harvie usually managed to smooth out any difficulties through an adroit exercise of diplomacy. "No one could have guided us in our formative stages with more intelligence, dedication and drive, and with complete diplomacy," noted Clarence Robinson. "I've seen bank presidents with a proposition before them and with their three points of view, and Harvie with great diplomacy and consideration would work out a solution so everybody was satisfied and happy. And as things worked out, it seemed that the Little Master had the right answer and the enterprise went on."

As Wilkinson had predicted to Paul Sackett, the prospect of obtaining the benefits of UVB's strength while retaining local autonomy helped the holding company acquire some of the most prestigious banks in its targeted market areas. Once the smaller "country" banks saw how the principle of a bank holding company operated in practice, they frequently dropped their opposition to the concept.

As they assessed prospects for expansion, Harvie and his colleagues were fortunate to be able to call upon the extensive experience of James Rawles, who had long
headed State-Planters' Correspondent Banking Department. Perhaps more than any
other banker in the Commonwealth, Rawles had a personal knowledge of the Virginia
banking community, and his guidance proved invaluable in selecting banks for acquisition based upon their stability and potential for future growth.

From the start, United Virginia focused upon two primary areas for expansion:
the Washington-Richmond-Norfolk corridor, and the major metropolitan areas of
western Virginia, from Winchester to Charlottesville and southward to Roanoke. "We
had a list of the desirable places where we wanted to be," recalled Paul Sackett, "and who
would be the best partners there." Accordingly, the first additional banks acquired by
UVB — each via merger with one the original affiliates — were Citizens National Bank
of Hampton (October 1964), the Shirlington Trust Company (May 1965), and the
Tri-County Bank in Hanover (August 1965). On December 31, 1965, the Peninsula
Bank and Trust Company of Williamsburg became the seventh affiliate bank, giving
UVB a total of 63 offices in 21 communities.

By the end of 1965, the holding company's assets had risen to nearly $650
million, and its loans had risen to over $387 million, an increase of more than 60 percent
over 1963. As Harvie Wilkinson had foreseen, the capital resources of United Virginia
Bankshares were vitally necessary to sustain Virginia's continued economic development,
for in the previous year 74 new manufacturing plants announced locations in Virginia,
while 94 existing firms declared their plans for expansion. Fueled by the rise in industrial
and commercial jobs opportunities, the state's unemployment rate had dropped to 2.8
percent, and Virginia now ranked as the second fastest growing state in the East.

Already Virginia was rapidly catching up to its neighbors to the south. It was no
wonder that Harvie reacted adversely to suggestions that UVB pay larger dividends to its
shareholders. "You want me to give away capital," he once protested to Paul Sackett,
"and that is the most valuable commodity we have."

When Harvie assumed his position as president and chief executive officer of
United Virginia Bankshares in January 1963, he realized that the affairs of the holding
company would require an increasing proportion of his time. Wilkinson therefore
resigned the presidency of State-Planters, which passed into the capable hands of

Edward F. Gee, who assumed the presidency of
State-Planters in 1963.

Edward Gee, though Harvie remained chairman of the bank's board of directors and
continued to participate actively in the affairs of State-Planters. In announcing the shift
in responsibilities, Harvie noted that "the duties of one person functioning as chief
executive of two growing corporations of the size of State-Planters and United Virginia
Bankshares have increased to such an extent that one can no longer do justice in the
discharge of his duties to either corporation… The holding company is now over $650
million in resources, and this dual responsibility should cease."

With their contrasting personalities and areas of expertise, Gee and Wilkinson
formed an effective management team. The firm of industrial psychologists — Rohrer,
Hibler & Replogle — whom Harvie had retained in the summer of 1964 to assess the
effectiveness of State-Planters' executive corps reported that Harvie's "venturesomeness"
and "warmth and congenial nature" was well balanced by Gee's "conservatism," "cool
analysis," and "objective nature."

In writing Harvie's own psychological evaluation, the consultants concluded that while he possessed "superior intellectual capacity," what made Harvie truly unique was his ability to employ *all* of his mental capabilities *all* of the time. Along the way, they also noted that "he augments his intellectual capacity with sound judgment, an intuitive understanding of people, and high drive… He is an exuberant, energetic, optimistic person who has set clear-cut, specific personal and business goals and persistently goes after them… He is highly skilled socially. He makes an immediate strong impact. His dominance, self-confidence, and skill are well 'laced' with a sense of humor and a sense of fairness."

On the other hand, the psychologists reported that Harvie was likely to lose intellectual efficiency "when he must attend to close detail or routine" (hence his need for organization — and completed staff work — so his mind would not be burdened with trivial matters), and that his enthusiasm, imagination, dominance, and charm "are exhilarating to his staff up to a point but beyond that point may seem to intimidate or discourage those who would like to emulate and, in fact, succeed him."

As chief executive officer and president of UVB, Harvie found it necessary to spend more time outside of Richmond, traveling to visit affiliate banks, and meeting with community leaders and presidents of other financial institutions. Accordingly, he delegated a great deal of detailed work at UVB and State-Planters to his subordinates, and yet he continued to closely monitor the pulse of both the holding company and the bank. Certainly there was no diminution in the volume of ideas — or "J.H.W., Jr. projects," as they came to be known — that poured out of Harvie's office.

Indeed, the same team of industrial psychologists reported that at State-Planters, "the flow of ideas is definitely from the top downward," due largely to "the super-abundance of ideas from the Chairman of the Board." At least one of Harvie's two secretaries could almost invariably be found at his side, ready to record suggestions, recommendations, or questions to which he wanted answers. James Wilson, the head of personnel at United Virginia Bankshares, recalled that "Harvie would walk around with a little IBM 'Think' book — just a little notepad with the word 'Think' on the front. And he'd always be making little notes. He'd come in to your office and take it out, and he'd flip it over and say, 'Last night I was thinking about you and this function, and here's something I'd like you to look into immediately.'"

For example, he came in one day in the early 1960s, and he said,

> "My boy, I want you to be in the forefront. We need a union readiness plan."
>
> "But Harvie," I said, "banks don't have unions."
>
> "I say," Harvie answered, "you don't seem to understand. Would you proceed to Hunton and Williams and get for me a union readiness plan?"

(And, in fact, years later Wilson did use the union readiness plan he drew up on that occasion.)

"Harvie's strength was in his breadth of vision, and his ideas, and his leadership of a group of people to get things implemented," confirmed Jack Jennings, who had succeeded Harvie as head of the State-Planters Investment Department. "He was persuasive enough that people would work very hard at what he wanted to do." Some of his suggestions, of course, turned out upon closer inspection to be impractical. According to Jennings, "Harvie had an idea a minute. He would try them out on Pat Patteson, and Pat would throw out 95 percent of them." For instance, Jennings had spent several years in the Virginia State Police in the early 1940s before returning to State-Planters in the postwar period, and Harvie decided that if Jennings had turned out so well, perhaps there was something valuable in the State Police training methods that he could turn to the advantage of the bank. When a second State Trooper proved to be considerably less capable, however, Harvie reluctantly concluded that Jennings was an exception.

Even as CEO of UVB and chairman of State-Planters, Harvie remained relatively accessible, available to give counsel to those who sought it. "Everybody knew he was smart," remarked Jack McElroy, who spent several years at State-Planters in the late 1950s before starting an investment banking career that later took him to the office of chairman and CEO of Wheat, First Securities. "He was friendly — he'd be walking around, and he'd stop and speak to you. He was sociable. He wasn't just sitting in his office behind a door."

Nor did Harvie stand upon formalities, despite his position and the respect that he engendered among subordinates. On a visit to Norfolk with Ed Gee in the mid-1960s, Harvie met for the first time several members of the senior management of UVB's recently-formed international division. When he arrived, one of the younger officers,

Charles Hays, walked up to Harvie and introduced himself, saying, "How do you do, Mr. Wilkinson, I'm Charles Hays." "No, no, my boy," Harvie replied briskly. "Call me 'Harvie.' You'll choke on it the first few times, but after that, you'll be all right."

Certainly Harvie made a conscious effort to know as many employees of State-Planters and UVB as possible. Jay and Lewis Wilkinson saw the effects of their father's concern for all the members of the State-Planters' family every Christmas Eve, when he took them down to the bank to introduce them to the staff and sing Christmas carols at the annual State-Planters holiday gathering. "You could tell with Dad that the person who operated the elevator was every bit as important to him as the senior vice president," observed Jay, "and that was because they belonged to this institution he cared so much about."

Still, Harvie had little tolerance for carelessness or mediocrity among his staff. "He had to fuss at a lot of people, but they didn't make the same mistake twice," remembered Mary Page Winberg, Harvie's long-time executive secretary and trusted friend. Nor did he particularly welcome disagreement from his subordinates, especially when he had already made his mind up. When faced with "picayune stubbornness," as he called it, Harvie's knuckles would turn white, and once, noted Jack Jennings, "he forbade all hostile comments for a minimum of twenty-four hours following the verbalization of his own expressed plans and philosophies. And thereafter if, according to Harvie, a downright stubborn opponent persisted he was then permitted to express a calm and dignified counter view."

Harvie's occasionally autocratic behavior was based primarily on his total dedication to the interests of United Virginia Bankshares. "Harvie combined his vocation and his avocation," explained Jennings, "and he hoped that people would be as enthusiastic about the bank and its prospects as he personally was." In an attempt to inspire UVB's board of directors to help the holding company drum up new business, Harvie sponsored an annual directors' meeting that usually lasted two to three days. "He would wine them, and dine them, and he would rev up the rhetoric," said Jennings. "You felt like you were in an old-fashioned revival. You got religion. He knew his powers of persuasion."

From time to time, Harvie personally produced a spectacular sort of entertainment to woo new clients for the bank. In the spring of 1962, for instance, he invited

Christmas Eve carol sing in the State-Planters lobby, 1959.

Right: Lewis Wilkinson joined in singing as he awaited the arrival of Santa Claus.

executives from corporations around the nation to be State-Planters' guests on a centennial tour retracing the progress of General George B. McClellan's "peninsula campaign" of April–July 1862. The guests assembled at State-Planters offices at Ninth and Main Streets in Richmond, and then set off by bus for Fort Monroe (a few miles east of Newport News) and a cruise in Hampton Roads, the site of the famous ironclad *Monitor-Merrimack* naval engagement. Following a luncheon on board the historic *Miss Ann*, the group proceeded to the five-star Williamsburg Inn in the late afternoon for a brief rest, followed by a reception, dinner, and a concert of period music by the Williamsburg Quintet.

Over the next three days, Harvie's guests enjoyed a tour of the Seven Days' battlefield area (hosted by renowned Civil War historian Clifford Dowdey); a guided tour of the restored area of Colonial Williamsburg, Jamestown, and nearby plantations; dinner at the King's Arms Tavern in Williamsburg; a visit to Berkeley Plantation — the home of presidents William Henry Harrison and Benjamin Harrison — and, to conclude the festivities, a luncheon at the Country Club of Virginia.

When he was not away on business trips, Harvie himself put in long days at the bank, often taking a colleague to lunch to learn more about developments in different departments, and frequently meeting with one or more officers after hours. But he clearly thrived on the challenge of making UVB work. Mary Page Winberg recalls that she *never* saw Harvie depressed. (Exasperated, perhaps, but never depressed.) "He would come in on Monday morning," she laughed, "and say, 'Boy, I just feel great!'"

With his hectic schedule, and his proclivity to constantly throw out new ideas like sparks from a wheel, one of the keys to Harvie's success was his well-known capacity for keeping every aspect of his life exceptionally well-organized. "His days were very carefully planned," recalled Robert Buford, the Hunton & Williams partner who succeeded Lewis Powell as UVB's general counsel. "When he got to the office, he knew what he was going to do all day long." His desk was covered with piles of memoranda and letters arranged so that he knew precisely which documents he had to get through by the end of the day, and he never went home until all that business had been successfully concluded.

Through it all, Harvie never lost his sense of humor. He enjoyed the Christmas parties at State-Planters, where junior members of the staff would perform satirical skits

"The Examiners" (from left to right) John T. Frawner,
Lewis B. Flinn, Jr., John A. Robertson, Louis C.
Einwick and Walter D. Tucker. A humorous skit after
the State-Planters annual Christmas Dinner, 1958.

Harvie and his colleagues checking their traditional
bow ties on Carlisle Davis Bow Tie Day, February 11,
1952. Inset is Harvie's "official" membership card.

VALIDATED:

This CERTIFIES that

J. Harvie Wilkinson, Jr.

having complied with all the tie-laws of this
association, is a member in good standing of the

CARLISLE-DAVIS-BOW-TIE-DAY

observed annually on the 11th day of February by the

STATE-PLANTERS BANK & TRUST COMPANY
RICHMOND, VIRGINIA

(Knot good unless validated by Carlisle Davis)

featuring the senior officers, and he participated in the bank's famous "Carlisle Davis Bow Tie Days," when, on Davis' birthday, everyone wore a bow tie in honor of his sartorial proclivities. And on Harvie's desk there reposed an ashtray, a souvenir from a vacation in Portugal. There was an inscription on the ashtray, but since it was written in Portugese, no one at the bank save Harvie knew that it said, "Neither a borrower nor a lender be." □

V

EDUCATION AND POLITICS

*"There is no life without society in mid-
twentieth century America, and politics is
society. There is no life without risk."*

— J. HARVIE WILKINSON, JR.

Throughout his years of service at State-Planters, Harvie Wilkinson had always willingly accepted the responsibility to become actively involved in the political and economic affairs of Virginia. Now, as head of the Commonwealth's largest financial institution, Harvie turned his sights outward, toward the national business scene, where he began to speak out on the critical issues confronting the American economy. Although he had earned a reputation as one of the leading progressives in the Virginia banking community, Wilkinson's views on national affairs revealed the conservative side of his nature, along with his predilection for fiscal soundness and stability.

One of the gravest threats to the nation's economic stability, in Wilkinson's view, was the constantly expanding federal deficit. Although the national debt in the early 1960s had not yet reached the appalling heights that it would scale three decades later, it was a measure of Harvie Wilkinson's foresight that he recognized the dangers of a spiralling deficit, and spoke out strongly in favor of efforts to put a ceiling on federal spending.

In a letter published in the *New York Times* on September 30, 1963, Harvie noted that the federal deficit was an issue "which ought to be causing all Americans great concern." "There is a high element of the incredible," he pointed out, "in the viewpoint that expenditures of over $90 billion have in them such upward rigidity that to hold the total at a given level is impossible, always barring a national emergency." To bring spending under control, Harvie suggested that "the President should propose to Congress a joint resolution limiting federal expenditures for each of the next three years to the 1962-63 level. It is vitally important that while we actively seek a deficit by cutting taxes, we proclaim firmly to the world that our pursuit of domestic growth will be restrained by fiscal prudence."

> This proposal by itself will not give the Federal Government a budgetary surplus, reduce the level of unemployment and bring our international accounts into balance. I do contend that once this basic elemental fact is addressed through action, we will have a foundation on the basis of which we can take other needed actions from a position of unassailable strength. Until we do, our position is weak and we are on the defensive.

On a closely related matter, Harvie strongly opposed a bid by Congressional liberals in late 1963 to scrap existing limits on the total supply of U. S. currency in operation. Specifically, Senators Paul Douglas (D., Ill.), and Jacob Javits (D., N.Y.), had advocated repeal of the long-standing federal statute that required the Federal Reserve System's gold supply to equal at least 25 percent of the system's currency in circulation, and at least 25 percent of the money deposited with the system by commercial banks. So strongly did Harvie feel about this issue that he agreed to testify before the Joint Economic Committee of Congress (which was chaired by Douglas) to defend the 25 percent rule, which Harvie described as an "impersonal restraint" on the Federal Reserve Board's power to expand the supply of money:

> Pressure must not be brought to bear on the Federal Reserve System to ease our monetary position any further. For too long now we have followed an easy money policy in the mistaken belief that this will encourage growth in our economy. History tells us that in any vigorous economy, good business means higher interest rates. The only thing that we have accomplished so far is to make this country a good place to borrow but a poor place to invest, both for foreigners and United States citizens.

"To change — or even talk about changing the present gold reserve requirement," Harvie argued, "is to suggest that we seek to escape our own self-imposed disciplines." "Like it or not," he replied, in response to a direct question from Senator Douglas, "out of man's long and tortuous history he has come to regard the gold reserve requirement as a form of restraint. If we were to cut it away…we would be deemed here and abroad to be escaping a discipline."

Instead, Harvie suggested that the Fed allow interest rates to rise while the government moved to moderate price and wage increases and stimulate investment. And in a bid to further reduce federal spending and encourage fiscal stability, he recommended that the United States "significantly reduce our foreign aid and dollar military expenditures abroad by demanding that those allies who have been made strong by our aid assume their fair share of the burdens we have been carrying almost alone."

Eighteen months later, the issue again arose when the flight of gold from the United States — prompted in large measure by an expansionary money policy, plus the growing American financial and military commitment to Southeast Asia — provoked alarm over the stability of the dollar. As a means of surmounting the immediate crisis, Wilkinson testified before the Senate Banking and Currency Committee in favor of the elimination of the 25 percent deposit reserve requirement, though he pointed out that the "submission of this bill to the Congress is a confession of failure to solve the balance of payments problem with which we have now been wrestling with only slight success for some years."

Yet Harvie made it clear that such a measure represented "merely the purchase of time — and expensive time it is." "We are such a great nation," Wilkinson added, "but, as is true of all humans, we seek to escape the disciplines which are imposed on us by the family, the local police force, the government, or the laws of economics." And if the nation continued to refuse to face its pressing economic problems — including the growing deficit — he warned that the United States would find itself "in the posture of a nation, powerful, strong, gone on a binge, and not too intelligent internationally."

While he sought to induce Congress to maintain a measure of fiscal sanity in its national economic policy, Harvie also strove to bring a more sophisticated understanding of the American economy to Virginia's school-age youth. In an address to the Richmond City School Board in January 1963, Wilkinson charged that "there is an abysmal ignorance of the historical American economic enterprise system" among the nation's high school students, as evidenced by the dispiriting results of research polls of graduating seniors across the nation. To remedy this appalling situation, Harvie urged the teachers, principals, supervisors, and administrative staff of Richmond's public schools to dedicate more time to explaining the history and nature of economics. He also offered concrete suggestions on methods to make the subject more understandable and interesting.

Combining his love of finance with a devotion to the cause of public education, Harvie followed up this proposal the following year with a projected comprehensive curriculum of economics for the Richmond school system. "The study of economics cannot be confined to the colleges," he pointed out, since not all of the city's high school graduates went on to institutions of higher learning. Indeed, Wilkinson warned that "approximately 70 percent of the oncoming generation will not have a knowledge of economics unless they acquire it in the secondary schools."

As far as Harvie was concerned, children could start learning the fundamentals of economics in grade school, perhaps by trading candy bars as part of a barter system. "I should be inclined to take them to a bakery," Harvie suggested, "and show them that when mother bought a loaf of bread she was hiring all the people in the bakery and the farmer who grew the wheat." Older elementary school students could study the interdependence of communities: "Richmond supports Detroit by buying automobiles; Detroit supports Richmond by buying cigarettes."

One can increase the breadth and complexity of economic concepts as the child moves through the high school years. Always the story will be the same, repeated in the language of the then current grade — history, human nature, economics — intertwined, interwoven and inextricable.

The Richmond school board adopted Harvie's recommendations, and in 1965-66 it supervised the design and implementation of the Developmental Economic Education Program. Specialists from the University of Virginia, in cooperation with teachers from the city school system, developed an economic curriculum that ranged from make-believe banks and stores in kindergarten, to the study of economic systems as an integral part of history and government classes in high school. Sponsored by the Joint Council on Economic Education, and funded in part by the Sears Foundation, the project was

September 1966: The Richmond School Board honors
Harvie for his years of service. Mrs. Hamilton
Crockford presided at the ceremony.

honored in 1967 by the National Education Association as Virginia's "Pacemaker"
program in educational improvement, "leading the way to better education for
America's youth."

Beyond instruction in economic theory, Wilkinson strongly urged that the
Richmond public school system adopt an ambitious program of vocational education "for
those who must have it and want it." In presenting the school board's vocational instruction proposal to the City Council in February 1964, Harvie warned that "economic
literacy and vocational education are becoming increasingly indispensable… On this
you may rely: we are either going to expand our educational assistance or we are going to
have a greater and greater welfare burden." Specifically, Wilkinson recommended that
the city construct two new facilities: a technical institute where high school graduates
could take two years of courses in modern technology; and a vocational-technical school
that would offer a broad variety of training programs aimed at employment in specific
industries.

Richmond's Trafficways Committee meets with City
Council to recommend the construction of a toll
expressway for the city, July, 1965.

As committed as he was to improving the quality of the Richmond system of
public education, Harvie found it impossible to continue to serve on the school board
when his original five-year term ended in September 1966, partly because his civic
responsibilities in other areas had continued to mount. In the autumn of 1963, Harvie
had consented to act as one of Governor Albertis Harrison's advisers on state economic
and budget affairs. Shortly thereafter, Harvie was elected chairman of the Virginia
Industrial Development Corporation, while he was already acting as chairman of the
Virginia Industrialization Group, an organization of business executives formed to help
speed up the state's economic growth. And in the spring of 1965, Wilkinson agreed to
serve on the City Council's Trafficways Committee, to find a way to ease the growing
auto traffic congestion in and around Richmond.

Most importantly, Harvie also accepted an appointment to serve a four-year
term, beginning in the spring of 1966, on the Board of Visitors of the University of
Virginia. The Board of Visitors — led by the Rector — acted as the school's governing

A gathering on the lawn at the University of Virginia before Harvie's first meeting as a member of the Board of Visitors. From left: President Edgar Shannon, Rector Frank W. Rogers, Former Governor Albertis S. Harrison, Jr., Mrs. E. Parker Brown, William M. Birdsong, and Harvie.

body, setting education policy and sharing the fiscal and fiduciary responsibility for the University. (This was not Harvie's first venture into the administration of higher education. Since 1953, he had been a member of the Board of Trustees of Hollins College, the alma mater of his wife, Letitia.)

The decade of the 1960s was an unusually turbulent time for the University of Virginia. With the rapid increase in the state's population, and the growing interest in higher education (partly as a result of the renewed emphasis on math and science instruction in the years immediately following the Sputnik affair), it seemed clear that the University would need to substantially expand its facilities if it were to continue to serve as the leading educational institution in the Commonwealth. The challenge, however, was to increase the student population without diluting the quality of education, a task that would require some serious soul-searching about the number of students the University could admit without losing its unique character.

"We started out with a long-range plan around 1962 that 10,000 would be our maximum," recalled Edgar F. Shannon, who served as president of the University from 1959 to 1972. Within a few years, however, the school had already reached the 10,000 mark, and was turning away thousands of applicants who were eminently qualified. Shannon then suggested that the University's Committee on the Future take another look at its projections, and the school later revised its figures upward to approximately 16,600 students.

Obviously this vast expansion in student enrollment required the Board of Visitors to find funds to build new classroom and housing facilities. At the same time, the Board embarked upon a campaign to attract eminent scholars to the University through public and private endowments and the formation of the Center for Advanced Studies, through which the level of the faculty in the social sciences and the humanities was significantly enhanced.

In April 1965, the University also formally established the Tayloe Murphy Institute, under the auspices of the Graduate School of Business Administration, to conduct research in the areas of public policy and economic development. The initial funds (eventually totalling one million dollars) to establish the Institute were donated by an admirer of the late Representative Murphy, a prominent Virginia business executive and politician who had died in 1962. But a condition of the donation was that these funds would be held in trust until another $600,000 had been raised through additional gifts.

Because the aims of the Tayloe Murphy Institute were very dear to the heart of Harvie Wilkinson, it was not surprising that Harvie was one of five Virginia businessmen who each contributed $25,000 in the fall of 1965 to help the Institute inaugurate its operations. Nor was that the full extent of Harvie's assistance. On December 8, 1965, the Board of Directors of State-Planters announced that it was celebrating the 100th birthday of the bank by making a donation of $100,000 toward the establishment of the Tayloe Murphy Institute.

For State-Planters, this substantial contribution was a means of celebrating the past — and showing the bank's appreciation of its present and former employees, executives, and customers — while saluting the future of the Commonwealth, and doing its part to ensure that Virginia would be well equipped to prosper in the coming decades.

Dean Charles C. Abbott (left) Harvie and President
Edgar F. Shannon, Jr., upon the presentation by
State-Planters of a $100,000 gift to the University of
Virginia Graduate School of Business Administration.

The bank's contribution provided a valuable impetus to the Institute's fund-raising efforts, and by early 1967, the requisite $600,000 had been obtained. On February 20, 1967, President Shannon officially declared the Institute operative.

On the social front, the University found itself confronting the issue of racial integration. Since 1951, the University had admitted blacks to its graduate professional schools; by 1960, it had begun admitting minorities to its undergraduate professional schools. The College of Arts and Sciences, however, was not integrated until the mid-1960s, and the issue of actively recruiting black undergraduates — and black faculty members — remained a sensitive one for years to come.

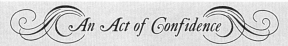

An Act of Confidence

THIS DAY marks the 100th birthday of the State-Planters Bank of Commerce and Trusts.

THE DIRECTORS of the Bank look forward confidently to the next 100 years and wish to salute the future with a meaningful contribution to the vitality of Virginia within the framework of whose history the Bank has had its life.

THE BANK owes much to all those who throughout the last 100 years have, by their loyalty, brought the Bank to its present stature.

THE DIRECTORS' appreciation both to those now gone and to present customers and friends may best be expressed by an act that should prove significant over the years ahead to their sons and daughters and to future generations of Virginians.

ANONYMOUS DONORS recently made a substantial starting gift toward the creation of the Tayloe Murphy Institute at the University of Virginia, to be operated under the auspices of its Graduate School of Business Administration, whose purposes will be to undertake studies that will include "any area of industrial and commercial development or of public policy that relates to such development."

THE DIRECTORS of the Bank are convinced of the urgent need for research dedicated to the economic advancement of Virginia and the prosperity of its people.

ACCORDINGLY, the Board of Directors of the Bank have voted to contribute $100,000 to the Institute and trusts that this action will encourage the realization of a great concept and the development of an Institute of vital importance.

FURTHERMORE it is hoped that this action will accelerate the date of the Institute's functioning and will also serve as an incentive to others who believe that the accumulated wisdom of generations should be applied to the problems of today and of the future.

BY ORDER OF THE BOARD OF DIRECTORS, STATE-PLANTERS BANK OF COMMERCE AND TRUSTS

PRESIDENT

CHAIRMAN OF THE BOARD

OUR FIRST 100 YEARS. In the past century, State-Planters has evolved from modest beginnings with capital of $200,000, to its present eminence with resources of over $350,000,000 and capital funds in excess of $26,000,000. The Bank's growth has paralleled the development of personal and business life in Virginia and in the Fifth Federal Reserve District to which it belongs, as well as in the nation at large.

Today, as a member of United Virginia Bankshares, State-Planters Bank in company with Citizens and Marine Bank (Newport News, Hampton and York County) First and Citizens National Bank (Alexandria, Arlington and Fairfax County) First National Trust and Savings Bank (Lynchburg) Merchants and Farmers Bank (Franklin) and The Vienna Trust Company (Vienna, Tysons Corner, McLean and Great Falls) constitute the foremost banking aggregate laboring with other banks in the State for its constructive development.

But size is transitory in a competitive society and it is attitude and action that count regardless of size. The Bank hopes by its actions to continue to serve the people of Virginia.

 State-Planters Bank of Commerce and Trusts
Richmond • Petersburg • Hopewell • Hanover County

In a full-page ad in the *Richmond Times-Dispatch*, State-Planters expresses its confidence in Virginia's future with a gift to help establish the Tayloe Murphy Institute at the University of Virginia.

The matter was further complicated by the fact that a number of official University functions were held at facilities that practiced discriminatory policies. Recognizing that this situation could be potentially embarrassing to the University, President Shannon made an administrative decision that the Board of Visitors could henceforth only conduct its business at establishments that were non-discriminatory. Although some members of the Board protested Shannon's decision, Harvie Wilkinson did not. "He spoke up very distinctly on this," Shannon recalled. "and said it was exactly right. He said it was the sort of thing they had to become aware of and sensitive to in the business world, and there was no question that it was right. Harvie was very clear, and very strong and helpful in that circumstance."

Several years later, the Board faced another controversy when it decided to admit women to the College of Arts and Sciences. It seemed perfectly clear to President Shannon, the Alumni Association, and a majority of the Board that the University could not escape its legal obligation to admit qualified female applicants, but the issue still generated a considerable amount of emotional reaction. While Harvie was prepared to vote in principle for the admission of women, he insisted upon thorough studies in advance of the cost of such a policy for the University. Since the Board had decided that the admission of women would not require a corresponding decline in the number of male students, it seemed clear that the advent of co-education was going to place a severe strain on the University's faculty and facilities. As Harvie stated in one of the Board's discussions on this issue, "the University was seeking to move forward on many fronts and inevitably there had to be priorities. And these priorities could not be set, he charged, "in the absence of good estimates on the cost of co-education."

On these and other issues, including his service as a member of the Finance Committee of the Board of Visitors, Harvie served as a staunch supporter of Shannon's efforts to enhance the academic strength and quality of the University. "In terms of educational values and aspirations of the University," noted Shannon, "he was very strong as a member of the Board and as an alumnus. And he just had such a very out-going, lively, and genial personality that I found him very stimulating right from the start." In 1970, at the end of his term on the Board, Harvie decided not to accept re-appointment in order to make room for his son Jay, who was appointed to the Board by Governor Linwood Holton. Throughout this period, Harvie remained active in the affairs of the Graduate School of Business Administration as well, encouraging support for the school among the state's business community.

During his term on the Board of Visitors, Harvie also spent considerable time seeking additional funding from the General Assembly for higher education in the Commonwealth. By that time, he was already a familiar figure on the Virginia political scene. Although Harvie harbored no political ambitions for himself, he firmly believed that his involvement in state politics was an integral part of his responsibility, and that of United Virginia Bankshares, as a concerned corporate citizen. In fact, he approved the formation of a corporate library in the United Virginia Bankshares offices to encourage his colleagues to keep pace with recent events in the political and financial world, and especially to stay abreast of trends affecting UVB's major customers. "The economics of man have become the handmaiden of politics, and accordingly it is essential to understand the political environment," he maintained. "We live as humans wrapped in political clothing. Whether the clothing is too heavy and suffocating is of overwhelming importance, for it is the human that will suffer."

Every other year, United Virginia Bankshares hosted a legislative dinner for key members of the General Assembly and many of the state's leading corporate executives. Usually the gatherings were held at the John Marshall Hotel in downtown Richmond. It was an opportunity for business and political officials to establish or renew personal contacts, and to exchange views on the issues currently confronting Virginia. "You felt honored to be included," remarked Mills Godwin, who came to Richmond as a freshman member of the legislature in 1948, and by 1963 was serving as lieutenant governor. "Those events were rather special. They were great social occasions, in that we always had a very elaborate social hour, and we had a chance to chat not only with Harvie, but with many of his friends."

After dinner, Harvie introduced the guest speaker — often another banker or corporate executive — who had been asked to speak on some aspect of Virginia's future. Occasionally the introduction itself was the highlight of the evening. "Harvie presided over these dinners in a remarkable way, with lots of humor," recalled Edgar Shannon. Mills Godwin agreed. "Harvie was always at his best in his introduction of his guest at these affairs," remarked Godwin, "and he did it in a way that only Harvie Wilkinson could do it — flamboyant, but very polished in his descriptive language. And it was always entertaining. He had enough humor and light-heartedness in it to make it interesting."

Indeed, it never took much prodding to persuade Harvie to stand before an audience and deliver his thoughts in the sort of well-polished, Churchillian cadences that one might have expected from a man who fervently admired the great British statesman. Although many of his speeches were carefully crafted in advance, he was equally gifted in speaking extemporaneously. "You could say, 'Harvie, tell us what you think of Japan,'" laughed Jack McElroy, "and he'd weave Japan in with Western Europe, and the United States, and the work ethic, and religion, and all sorts of things, and you'd think he had worked for three days on the speech." Harvie once described his own technique in speaking extemporaneously as "simply throwing in a few subordinate clauses while he thought of what he was going to say next." More seriously, a long-time associate characterized Harvie's speeches as "full of colorful language, good at imagery and arresting figures of speech, inspirational, and finally, capable of projecting the speaker as equally attractive at a meeting of the NAACP or at a gathering of the Society of the Cincinnati," to which Harvie did, in fact, belong.

Harvie's political philosophy probably could best be characterized as "constructive conservatism." "The constructive conservative," he claimed, "weighs human nature and the individual human being a good deal more heavily in the scales than does his liberal counterpart. The conservative feels human nature changes but slowly, and he does not feel that a person in authority in government is automatically endowed with either the virtues or the wisdom of the angels."

When he applied this philosophy to practical issues, Harvie generally combined a progressive (though certainly not radical) stance on social issues with a staunchly conservative attitude in fiscal affairs. He frequently supported the Byrd organization, and had immense respect for Senator Harry F. Byrd Sr.'s integrity and sense of fiscal responsibility, and for the Senator's tremendous contributions to the Commonwealth. Yet Harvie was not averse to breaking with the Byrd organization when he felt it was too autocratic or inflexible, as indeed he had done during the massive resistance controversy.

Not surprisingly, Harvie also became close personal friends with Governor Albertis Harrison and his successor, Mills Godwin. Both Harrison and Godwin shared Harvie's views on the importance of industrial development for Virginia's future, a

Virginia's first Trade Mission to Europe, 1967. Harvie is
on the left, Governor Mills Godwin, fourth from left.

subject which they occasionally discussed — along with other less weighty matters —
over dinner at the Wilkinson house or at the Governor's mansion. "We developed a good
friendship," Godwin said years later. "Harvie didn't always agree with me on everything
of a political nature, but he was very frank in stating his views and the reasons for his
views, and I respected his judgment."

Governor Harrison had inaugurated the state's industrial development program,
and Godwin continued to advance the cause of economic expansion during his first term
as chief executive of the Commonwealth (1966-70). To that end, Governor Godwin
personally led the first Virginia Trade Mission to Europe in March 1967, "to project the
image of the state and all of its advantages in competition with the images of the other
49 states." Not surprisingly, Godwin appointed Harvie as a member of the mission; in
fact, Godwin credits Harvie with being one of the chief architects of the project.

The Virginia Chamber of Commerce sponsored the trip, a 21-day tour of conferences and meetings with officials in Belgium, Italy, Spain, Switzerland, Scandinavia, and

the United Kingdom. As Harvie himself later recalled, "The purpose of the mission was three-fold — first, to sell and make known Virginia products," especially coal, seafood, feed cattle, furniture, and specialty items.

> Second [continued Harvie], we were interested in developing awareness on the part of Europeans and increasing their use of the great port of Hampton Roads (embracing the ports of Norfolk, Portsmouth, and Newport News). Lastly, but by no means least, we were interested in making known the advantages of Virginia to foreign corporations who might want to locate plants in the United States, and we wished very much to increase tourist travel to Virginia.

The mission proved to be extraordinarily successful in stimulating interest in Virginia among western European nations. In time, programs that grew out of the mission produced 12,000 new jobs and over $450 million in investments in Virginia by foreign firms. The trip also provided Harvie with an opportunity to acquaint his colleagues with the finer points of the continent's culture and cuisine. He and Letitia had visited Europe on numerous occasions, and so Harvie served as a sort of unofficial grand master for the tour, organizing dinner parties and evening events, and keeping everyone in good spirits. He even persuaded the members of the mission to bring a tuxedo on the trip, so they could have at least one black-tie dinner before they departed for home.

At La Scala in Milan, Harvie and several of his colleagues attended a performance of *Il Trovatore*; "it is a beautiful opera house," he wrote, "and very awe-inspiring." The entire mission saw a production of *Swan Lake* in Stockholm, and four of them also attended *Faust* in Brussels, performed on a circular stage. And always there was good food and fine wine. "We had so much food in lunches and dinners that I know full well how the Hungarian geese must feel when they are being prepared for *pâté maison*," Harvie said. In Brussels, the final stop on the tour, Harvie gave a banquet for the entire Mission where, in his words, "we reviewed the happenings of our trip and took an oath with hands upraised to tell no one [of their indulgences] after we touched down at Dulles."

Ironically, Harvie's roommate for most of the tour was Robert L. Gordon, president of First and Merchants' Bank, UVB's primary competitor. The other members of the mission joked that the two bankers had arranged to room together so each could keep an eye on the other.

Governor Godwin's other major contribution to the Commonwealth's economic development was the rescinding of Virginia's long-standing constitutional prohibition against the issuance of general obligation bonds to finance capital improvements. Since 1924, Virginia had labored under the burden of a "pay-as-you-go" plan, which severely limited the state government's ability to fund construction of highways, college classrooms and dormitories, and hospitals. Beginning in the early 1960s, however, the rate of population growth in Virginia had begun to skyrocket, and it showed no signs of slowing. Capital expenditures fell far behind needs, with deleterious consequences to the state's education, health, recreation, and transportation facilities. For instance, Virginia ranked 50th among the states in its capital outlays for health and welfare; 21st in capital outlays for highways despite the fact that the state ranked 15th in population; and only 27 percent of the state's college-age population were in Virginia colleges, compared with 35 percent for the South and 47 percent for the nation as a whole.

To remedy this disquieting situation, Governor Godwin proposed in 1966 an amendment to the state constitution to permit Virginia to issue general obligation bonds. To generate popular support for the measure, Godwin arranged a series of regional educational conferences throughout the state, where he and other distinguished business and political leaders could explain their position in detail. Given his recognition of the need for continued development throughout the state, it was not surprising that Harvie Wilkinson was one of the foremost advocates of the bond amendment. As Edgar Shannon later observed, "With good business practices, you've got to invest, and do capital outlay. You've got to borrow some money that you know is going to pay off." Accordingly, Harvie volunteered to appear as the keynote speaker at the governor's eighth and final conference, held in Alexandria, in northern Virginia, on March 5, 1967.

In his speech that evening, Harvie pointed out that the state was already spending approximately $100 million out of general fund revenues for fixed capital purposes. That was bad enough; but in the near future, Harvie predicted, Virginia inevitably would face an imposing surge in operating costs for such items as maintenance and administrative expenses, and schoolteachers' and professors' salaries. And Harvie warned that "nothing like $100 million will be available hereafter for such purposes out of the general fund." He proposed, instead, that the General Assembly appoint a committee

Richmond Times-Dispatch

'Pay-as-You-Go' Held Restraining Education Progress

By Robert Holland
Times-Dispatch
Education Writer

ALEXANDRIA — The state's pay-as-you-go policy of financing schools and other public services was challenged by a Richmond banking executive and strongly criticized by Northern Virginia leaders at an education conference here yesterday.

Selection procedures for the state superintendent of public instruction and county school boards also were attacked.

J. Harvie Wilkinson Jr. of Richmond said he has become "increasingly persuaded that the state Constitution must be amended to permit the issuance of state debt under proper conditions."

850 Attend

His remark won hearty applause from some 850 participants in the last of eight regional conferences on education, which have been held as follow-ups to Gov. Mills E. Godwin ... Education in ...

mas C. Boushall, had propos... the state Constitution be "pr... amended to allow state bo... public school purposes.

Wilkinson, chairman of t... of State-Planters Bank of C... and Trusts, suggested that... eral Assembly appoint a c... in 1968 "to examine capit... erating needs for the next... and to study requisite saf... amending th... her stat... will mean "... ing $100 r... larger amo... can be ded... in the futu...

Gov. ... mitted to... his spe... mented ... as he F... ferenc... $50 r... enue ... cent ... "pit ... tior ...

State 'Pay-as-You-Go' Policy Hit at Education Conference

come in one of three ways: Underwriting borrowing by school boards, state school bond referendums or an increase in the State Literary Fund program by which loans are made for school construction.

In most school divisions, he added, school board members are selected by school trustee electoral boards, which are appointed by circuit court judges. "In effect, this removes the school board from accountability to the people," he said.

O. U. Johansen, principal of Washington-Lee High School in Arlington, agreed: "It is my belief that Virginia is in the lowest quartile of states in support of schools not as a ... nort of citi-

ton School Supt. Ray Reid was applauded when he declared, "The localities must impress upon the state the need for better textbooks in our schools." He said the State Department of Education's method of buying and distributing books needs reevaluation.

Joseph B. Johnson, a member of the Prince William County Board of Supervisors, said the state's lack of a capital improvement and debt service program for local schools means localities forced to incur heavy debts to build schools "have in effect been penalized."

He also urged that the state school aid formula be based on average daily membership of pupil instead of average daily attendance ... dor the ADA formula, he

The News-Virginian

Established 1892
Your HOME Newspaper Dedicated to Serving YOU

Waynesboro, Virginia, 22980, Tuesday, October 8, 1968

Accomplishments Reviewed:

Support Of Bond Issue Is Urged At Annual C Of C Meeting Here

"Either we are masters of our pursestrings or slaves to the pursestrings of another."

This statement climaxed an appeal for support of the $81 million statewide bond issue made by J. Harvie Wilkinson Jr. of Richmond at the 46th annual banquet of the Waynesboro East August Chamber of Commerce Monday night at Gen-

ties, he cited the fact that 27 per cent of Virginians in the age range of 18 to 25 years are in college, and compared this with the 37 per cent figure in the South and 48 per cent figure in the nation. This, too, is not in the tradition of the Commonwealth, he said.

If the bond issue is not approved, Mr. Wilkinson said, its defeat ...

a wealthy state and a conservative people." Virginia is 14th among the 50 states in personal income, he said. It is 15th in population, and 16th in value of materials used in the production of goods that go into the manufacturing processes.

"Virginians are able to pay for what they want, according to their ... erted.

Support of Bond Issue I[s] At Annual C of C Meeti[ng]

(Continued From Page 1)

ing states in education, parks and roads," he said. "Ask yourself: as one votes yes or no on this issue, he is also voting yes or no as to whether Virginia is to be a competitive leader among the states, or a second-rate follower. Ask: Do I want my children to have the best opportunity possible? And, Do I want the Commonwealth to be a leader, or do I want it to default?"

Mr. Wilkinson was introduced by Malcolm G. Jones Jr., first vice president of the Chamber.

Reviewing the accomplishments of the year, Chamber President Edward P. Berlin Jr. said that the most significant was the creation of the Economic Development Corpora-

coming to the area at isting ones in their de

Another accomplishment ... nificance, he said, was the initiation of the first annual Fall Foliage Festival "born and coordinated by the Chamber." The Festival begins with a parade at 6 p.m. Wednesday.

Mr. Berlin said that during the year, brochures on Waynesboro for tourists have been revised and reprinted at a cost of some $700.

One of the most surprising projects of the year, he said, was the seminar for women drivers. "We expected maybe 30 women to turn up," he said, "and were astonished that 163 women actually attended the seminar."

Providing information for local

Berlin said

The maj
the Chamb
the preside
not as large
of this size,
the budget
tential of t

Seven r
the Chaml
are: G. Le
architect;
Pont Co.
Gordon of
Inc.; Quent
Shenandoa
of First at

Back Bond Issue, Richmond Banker Urges State COC

By Ozzie Osborne
World-News Political Writer

Virginia businessmen today were urged to become involved in matters usually handled by government and to support the $81 million bond issue Nov. 5.

A strong plea for approval of the bond issue was made by J. Harvie

He said, too, that businessmen must be shown where they can profitably solve urban problems. Otherwise, he said, any work they undertake will be only a "charity-type thing."

Clem D. Johnston of Roanoke a former president of the U.S. Chamber of Commerce, was panel mod-

Newspaper articles noted Harvie's energetic campaign for a constitutional amendment to permit the Commonwealth to issue $81 million in bonds.

"to examine capital and operating needs for the next four years and to study requisite safeguards in amending the Constitution of Virginia to permit issuance of direct debt."

In an editorial on the bond issue controversy, the *Richmond Times-Dispatch* termed Wilkinson's support of the administration's amendment "the haymaker in a devastating one-two punch," the first half of which had been delivered previously by Thomas Boushall in a conference in Richmond. "Here are two of the leading bankers in this part of the United States," the editorial continued, "urging issuance of bonds as the truly conservative course for Virginia. It is noteworthy that the audience broke into loud applause when each man delivered his appeal."

Several months later, Harvie published a more extensive analysis — and an even more fervent defense — of the benefits of the general bond amendment in the December 1967 issue of Commonwealth magazine. Calling Virginia "an island of pay-as-you-go in the midst of competition" from neighboring states that permitted borrowing for capital outlay projects, Harvie began by noting that current capital outlay requests from state agencies totalled $416 million per year, nearly double the annual outlays for the past six years. These, Harvie explained, were realistic estimates prepared by professionals; "They are not the fabrication of a Jules Verne dream world but bring us face to face with stark reality."

But the real crunch, Harvie argued, would come over the next six years, since total capital outlays from both general and special funds would total $2,498 million, against projections of net income that totalled only $1,925 million. "If we continue our present pay-as-you-go basis, will there be enough money for capital expenditures?" he asked. "The answer is a resounding no!" Besides, the issuance of general bonds made sense from a sound fiscal standpoint as well, since the cost of building new classrooms and hospitals was rising at an average of nearly 5 percent each year. "Even in today's money market," Wilkinson said, "Virginia could borrow, for example, at less than 4.3 percent for eight years, thus saving money [$50 million] by borrowing and building now rather than suffering the rising costs of the future. Of equal importance…we would have the capital facilities for the benefit and use of our people immediately."

"The most sensible option," Harvie concluded, "is to pay for the capital outlay deficiency out of the proceeds of full faith and credit bonds issued by the state. A bright future for Virginia and the best interest of its citizens depend upon it." His arguments

Harvie with Letitia receiving a Steuben glass creation, "Bird In Flight," in recognition of his service as President of the Association of Registered Bank Holding Companies, 1969-70. Presenting the award is George S. Eccles, President of First Security Corporation, Salt Lake City.

proved persuasive. In the ensuing referendum, Virginians voted overwhelmingly to authorize the sale of $81 million in bonds for higher education and mental health facilities.

Harvie's deepening responsibilities in the fields of state politics and education brought no diminution of his involvement in the corporate community. He remained active in the affairs of the American Bankers Association, serving on the ABA's federal legislative committee and its state bank research committee. In 1967, Harvie was appointed a member of the Federal Advisory Council, the body which formally advised the Board of Governors of the Federal Reserve System on financial matters. As a representative of the Fifth Federal Reserve District, he was reappointed to the Council in 1968 — serving as its vice president for a year — and again in 1969. He also served on the Advisory Committee of the Federal Deposit Insurance Corporation, and chaired the committee on federal relationships of the Association of Reserve City Bankers.

The Board of Directors of Media General Corporation, 1976. From left to right: John Stewart Bryan III, Andrew J. Brent, Paul E. Manheim, Alan S. Donnahoe, D. Tennant Bryan, J. Harvie Wilkinson, Jr., Gordon Gray and Archie K. Davis.

In the spring of 1969, Harvie was elected president of the Association of Registered Bank Holding Companies. He considered this honor extremely significant, given the prominence and stature of this national banking organization. Certainly Harvie spared no effort in displaying the historical and culinary virtues of Virginia to his colleagues in the association. When he hosted the annual gathering of the Association's representatives, Harvie arranged a special outdoor luncheon on the grounds of Westover Plantation, catered by the chefs of Colonial Williamsburg. The weather, of course, cooperated splendidly, as it usually did for Harvie's events.

Between 1964 and 1970, Harvie consented to serve on the board of directors of numerous major corporations, including Freeport Minerals Company, Media General, Inc. (whose newspaper holdings included the *Richmond News Leader* and the *Richmond Times-Dispatch*, among others), Lawyers Title Insurance Corporation, Miller & Rhoads, and Richmond Hotels, Inc. His longest term of service, however, was the twenty-five years he spent as a director of Philip Morris.

It was during Wilkinson's tenure on the Philip Morris board that the company became the largest employer in Virginia, with a huge research facility and a 1.2 million square foot operations plant — the largest cigarette manufacturing facility in the world — along Interstate 95 outside of Richmond. By the late 1960s, Philip Morris was also one of the leading buyers of the state's tobacco crop.

"Harvie had all the courtly manners of a southern gentleman, very intelligent, very outspoken, and very articulate," observed Joseph Cullman, who became president of Philip Morris in late 1957, at approximately the same time that Wilkinson became a member of its board of directors. (Harvie actually had been asked to join the board by Cullman's predecessor, who died shortly thereafter during a sudden illness. Harvie offered to step aside if the new president wished to make a different appointment, but Cullman insisted that Harvie's expertise would be invaluable on the board.) Years later, Cullman recalled that Harvie was a force on the board right from the start, never hesitating to give his opinion on issues facing the company. Although his advice was especially valuable on financial matters, Cullman noted that Harvie's opinions on a wide range of problems — always supported by logic and evidence — carried great weight with the other members of the board.

Unlike his activities on behalf of economic development in Virginia, where he frequently found himself leading his more conservative colleagues toward the future, Harvie Wilkinson acted as a stabilizing influence on the plans of Philip Morris' management. The company was growing so rapidly during the 1960s and 1970s, expanding its operations and acquiring other tobacco companies, that it benefited from what Cullman termed Harvie's "constructive restraining influence." "Harvie gave us financial sophistication, and a certain conservative attitude toward things that he always maintained," said Cullman. On the other hand, Harvie never allowed himself to be bound by precedent when a bold approach seemed to be called for. Cliff Goldsmith, a former president of Philip Morris, once told Harvie's son, Lewis, that "your father is very unique, because I have never heard him say, 'That isn't the way we used to do it.'" Each time Harvie attempted to retire from the board of directors, the company asked him to stay, or at least remain on its advisory board. "If I had to pick out one director during my career who was the most influential," concluded Cullman, "I'd say Harvie Wilkinson."

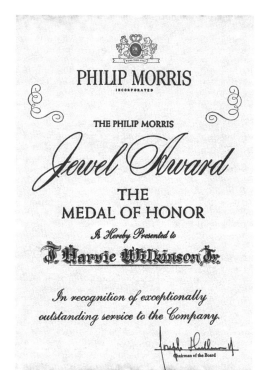

Philip Morris bestowed its highest honor, the Jewel
Award, to Harvie "for truly exceptional accomplishments and dedicated service."

Harvie entertaining the Philip Morris Board of
Directors with his post-prandial eloquence at a meeting
in 1970. From left to right: David E. Satterfield, Jr.,
J. Harvie Wilkinson, Jr., Joseph F. Cullman III,
Gordon L. Crenshaw and George Weissman.

Since Philip Morris' administrative headquarters were located in Manhattan, the meetings of the board of directors gave him an opportunity to revisit New York City on a regular basis. In fact, Harvie had always made a special effort to keep the lines of communication open with his friends and financial associates on Wall Street, visiting the major banks there at least three or four times a year to stay abreast of their activities. As he once explained to one of his Richmond colleagues, it was absolutely essential to understand what the decision-makers in the New York banks were doing. "They may not always be right," Harvie acknowledged, "but what they are doing will make markets move, one way or the other."

For those who knew him primarily as a Richmond banker, Harvie's familiarity with the movers and shakers on Wall Street could come as something of a surprise. Early in his career as an attorney with the law firm of Hunton, Williams, Gay, Powell, and Gibson, Robert Buford accompanied Wilkinson on a business trip to New York. "I was very much impressed with the way Harvie — the country banker, if you will — could maneuver around Wall Street," noted Buford. "I remember one time when we borrowed $15 million on nothing more than a handshake. That was the way business was done in those days."

This same urbane, sophisticated financier who moved so easily among the nation's leading bankers on Wall Street could also wax poetic over the demolition of an office building across the Street from United Virginia's offices in downtown Richmond. In the summer of 1965, the Ebel Building (at the northwest corner of 9th and Main Streets), which formerly housed a variety of small businesses — a cigar store, a lunch counter, and an engraving plant, among others — was razed to make way for a new bank headquarters, and Harvie's eulogy to the dismembered structure found its way into a local column in the *Richmond News Leader*. The final stanza of the poem was perhaps the most eloquent:

> I used to stand so proudly.
>
> Foundations, opened to the heavens, are dried and cleansed by rays of summer's sun.
>
> Another building begins its rise — to start its own life process.
>
> My spirit shall be with this structure, new, but I shall laugh;
>
> She, too, will in God's good time return to dust —Buildings are like humans.

One might readily acknowledge that J. Harvie Wilkinson, Jr. was no Percy Bysshe Shelley, but by the same token, Shelley was no Wilkinson, either. Having discovered an audience for his literary endeavors, Harvie accepted an occasional invitation to serve as a guest columnist in the *News Leader*. His columns varied from trenchant observations upon relevant social and political topics to whimsical ruminations upon matters of more philosophical or cultural import. A few excerpts should provide a flavor of the Wilkinson style:

> We are all creatures of habit and the older we get the more ingrained our habits tend to become. Generally, we go to work the same route and return from work, maybe by a different route — because of one-way streets — but basically it is the same. We carve a pattern like grooving a bar of soap with a nail file. What a pity! How do we ever get to know Our Town? Two blocks off of my groove to work there is going on what seems to be a self-propelled rehabilitation of an area that was surely headed downward with all its cancerous implications for the neighborhood. But alas, I did not see this until a fire one morning forced me to take a detour. So much in the groove was I!

> Men are the weaker sex in so many ways; we do indeed need our own lib movement. We do not have guile. We do not plot all day how to handle our wives in the evening for the effectuation of Machiavellian-laid plans. We are a bit silly where women are concerned even though from time to time we may be bemused.

> The most delectable of vegetables when at its prime is awesomely abused because its color is red. In its prime, the tomato has beautiful color and is tasty indeed. Its acidity, when broiled without bread crumbs, is delectable. When baked with artfulness, it is choice food. For us in Richmond, the Hanover tomato is the epitome of all the virtues for this product.

> Now comes the abuse. Because of its color and shipments from the garden states during the winter, there is a very widespread tendency to serve this vegetable either sliced or in quarters in salads as decor. Anyone who has eaten one of these fall-winter tomatoes gags upon recollection of the Hanover County product. The taste is nonexistent, and the pith has a repellent quality…

By the end of 1969, UVB consisted of ten affiliate banks, with a total of 98 offices in 31 communities across the state. The most significant addition was the Seaboard Citizens National Bank, which gave UVB a presence for the first time in the vital Norfolk market. Because it seemed likely that the Federal Reserve Board — which still maintained an extremely conservative attitude toward the expansion of bank holding companies on anti-trust grounds — might have rejected UVB's application to acquire Seaboard, Wilkinson was persuaded to apply for approval through the Comptroller of the Currency, who had statutory authority to supervise the Nation's national banks. The incumbent comptroller, James Saxon, was known to be sympathetic to bank growth by consolidation; however, Saxon had already announced his intention to retire from office on November 9, 1966, and so the UVB staff had to work with extreme haste. Over the next several months, a plan was developed to consolidate Seaboard with UVB's affiliate, Merchants and Farmers Bank of Franklin, under a national charter. The consolidation was approved on November 8, one day before Saxon left office.

Harvie later acknowledged that the acquisition of Seaboard was "the greatest feat once [UVB] came to birth." "If we had not been able to affiliate with Norfolk at the time we did, in my judgment we would have been forever foreclosed except for borning a child de novo," he claimed. "Instead, we have partners of great character and great capacity."

Earlier that year, while he was traveling through Europe with Governor Godwin's trade mission, Harvie Wilkinson had begun to formulate a plan to establish a foreign banking subsidiary for UVB. It was clear to Harvie that such a bank would be extremely useful in financing international transactions if the Commonwealth wished to promote commerce between Virginia corporations and their foreign trading partners. Not only would a foreign subsidiary preclude the need to go outside the state for capital, but it would also promote the use of the Hampton Roads ports as well as the ports of Richmond, Hopewell, and Alexandria. The Federal Reserve Board gave its approval in February 1968, and on April 1 of the same year, United Virginia Bank International — the first such bank in the Commonwealth — commenced operations from its headquarters in Norfolk, offering a wide range of services that included foreign exchange, export financing, and letters of credit.

UVB and its affiliates were somewhat more cautious in entering the rapidly-growing consumer credit market in the mid-to late 1960s. After completing exhaustive

The new headquarters building of UVB's Norfolk
affiliate, Seaboard-National, with Harvie speaking
at the opening ceremonies in April 1970.

studies of the emerging bank credit card industry, UVB finally issued its first VISA cards in September 1968. One month later, the holding company entered the mortgage banking business with the acquisition of the Investment Corporation of Norfolk, thereby significantly enhancing United Virginia's capacity for real estate lending.

Wilkinson obviously relished the opportunity to expand UVB's range of services to the public. Virginia's population was continuing to grow nearly 50 percent faster than the nation as a whole, with a corresponding boost in personal income to nearly $14 billion in 1968. As the state's largest banking institution, UVB certainly gathered its share of the consumer market, but Harvie was always searching for ways to increase the public's acceptance and recognition of United Virginia Bankshares and its affiliates. Accordingly, State-Planters sponsored an advertising campaign that sought to alter the traditional public perception of bankers as austere and rather formal individuals. "We're a first-name kind of bank," ran one State-Planters advertisement. "So, even if your man from State-Planters is saddled with a name like Horatio, he'd like you to use it." Well, this was fine for most of the bank officers, but the advertisement aroused considerable speculation in the press as to exactly what J. Harvie Wilkinson's first name really was. (It was "James," of course. Interestingly, the presidents of three of Richmond's other leading banks also used only the initial "J." for their first name.)

In a more serious vein, Harvie devoted a considerable measure of his time as chairman of UVB to the challenge of integrating and focusing the operations of the affiliate banks. As one senior bank officer noted, "He recognized that you had to have a game plan, and that you had to direct and coordinate your efforts." By the late 1960s, as the leaders of each of the affiliate banks came to accept the advantages of centralized operations, UVB had gone far toward coordinating the banks' marketing, auditing, bookkeeping and purchasing functions, while converting their computing facilities to a single configuration.

As UVB moved closer toward the ideal of an administratively unified bank, it seemed time to establish a common name for all the affiliate banks and branches. Besides simplifying the holding company's marketing and advertising efforts, Harvie realized that the adoption of a common name would signify the company's presence throughout Virginia, and help develop public awareness of the various affiliates as part of the holding company. This consideration took on added importance as Virginia's population became increasingly mobile. By the end of the 1960s, approximately 20 percent of the state's residents moved to new jobs or residences every year, frequently relocating within the state. "We didn't want to lose somebody in Lynchburg if he moved to Northern Virginia," Wilkinson explained. "The best way to do that was to have a common name."

So Harvie retained the New York consulting firm of Lippincott & Margulies, Inc. to evaluate the bank and its markets, and propose a new name for the holding company. For several months, Lippincott and Margulies attempted to generate names that would meet UVB's criteria: a distinctive and desirable image connoting strength, competence, and widespread operations; visual appeal; and compatibility with the affiliate bank designations. Among the final recommendations of the consultants were such names as Heritage, Horizon, Landmark, Patriot, Sovereign, and a host of names attempting to incorporate the first syllable of "Virginia" — Virbank, Virginiad, Viridian, and Virnia.

After hearing Lippincott and Margulies' presentations and considering all the proposed alternatives, Ed Gee suddenly recommended to Harvie that they throw them all out. Gee argued, quite cogently, that wholesale change would create nothing but confusion, "endless explanations, endless mystification, and endless disagreements with our total break with the past." "I'm convinced," Gee wrote to Wilkinson on March 21, 1968, "that we should forget about bridge-names, state-related names, strength-names, image-names, or coined-names, and agree promptly on the sensible, solid, common name we have had available all along: 'United Virginia Bank,'" followed by a hyphen and the affiliate bank name.

Harvie agreed. "I want you to know," he announced to the team of consultants, "that 'United' is not going, and 'Virginia' is not going. 'United' stands for strength, and 'Virginia' stands for integrity." And the longer he thought about it, the less Harvie liked the idea of a brand new name. "I've worked too hard with the investment bankers and Wall Street getting our name known to give it up," he decided.

Instead, the UVB board decided to adopt Gee's recommendation to add "United Virginia Bank" to the front of each affiliate bank's name, with a suffix indicating its geographic location or former title. First National Lynchburg, for instance, became known as United Virginia Bank/First National. It was an action that marked a significant milestone in the transition of UVB from a loosely-structured holding company to one

Unveiling the handsome, new UVB logo on February 19, 1969.

single bank. As Harvie Wilkinson explained at the ceremony to unveil the holding company's new logo on February 19, 1969, "This identifying separatism tells the public that we are a statewide banking system capable of offering the most sophisticated banking services, while at the same time retaining a local identity. Here in Richmond, there is no longer a State-Planters Bank of Commerce and Trusts. As of now, there is United Virginia Bank/State-Planters." ☐

VI

VALEDICTORY

"You need the sustenance that comes
from plowing up some good new earth.
Going over the same rabbit path is not
much fun."

— J. HARVIE WILKINSON, JR.

In the spring of 1970, Harvie Wilkinson announced that he would retire as president
and chief executive officer of United Virginia Bankshares, and chairman of the board of
UVB/State-Planters, on April 30, 1971. More than any other single individual, Harvie
had been responsible for the creation of United Virginia Bankshares. It was his inspira-
tion and formidable determination that had brought the holding company into existence,
and he had guided and nurtured it with a strong, capable hand through its early and
formative years. He had led the transformation of UVB from a loosely-structured establishment with assets of $454 million into a nationally respected financial organization
controlling resources of more than $1.3 billion. Now, as Wilkinson approached his
sixty-fifth birthday, it was time to step aside for the next generation of leadership.

Someone once asked Harvie if he approved of mandatory retirement at the age
of 65. "Absolutely," he replied without hesitation. "The line administration must ever be
kept fresh and vital. It is essential that as men reach a given age they get out of the line
and let younger men with their ideas, hopefully different from the ideas of their
predecessors, take over." For his successor as chief executive officer at United Virginia
Bankshares, Harvie selected Kenneth A. Randall, former chairman of the Federal Deposit

Taking a few moments to share his thoughts with an
interviewer shortly before his retirement.

Insurance Corporation. Ed Gee would succeed Harvie as chairman of the board of UVB/State-Planters, while Jack Jennings took over as president and CEO of the bank.

Shortly before he retired, Wilkinson delivered one of the most prescient speeches of his career. Speaking to a gathering of the Richmond Rotary Club, Harvie surveyed the state of contemporary society both at home and abroad, and, with the wisdom of more than forty years' experience in the nation's financial markets, warned of the impending dangers of inflation and unemployment, with all their concomitant deleterious effects upon the stability of governments. But Harvie's analysis ran further and deeper than economics alone. "Our people are increasingly demanding," he observed, in tones reminiscent of Henry Adam's famous critique of modern society more than sixty years earlier:

> We are living in one of the most demanding eras mankind has ever experienced. How fast can society and its institutions adjust to the satisfaction of these demands? The velocity of history is the single greatest problem of our age. Never before has so much happened in such short time spans…
>
> One is tempted to be drowned in pessimism if he looks at the short-run history of our lifetime and yet each generation is but a member of a relay team in the march of mankind…
>
> We are going through in our own society and in the society of the Western World wrenching changes in structure. In the developing nations of Africa, South America and the Orient equally cataclysmic changes are taking and will take place.

As he neared the date of his retirement, Harvie also shared with his colleagues his thoughts on the future of banking in the United States and abroad. "We shall cross state lines," he predicted accurately. "The holding company will be the mechanism. Banks under $20 million in ten years you may count on your fingers and toes. We are in a great historical cycle. The power of the economics of life over the political power always win in the long run… We will have a European common market, we will have a European currency. We will eventually have a single currency in the Atlantic union… The banker of the future will be a businessman. He will not be an investment man as I was, he will not be a credit man, he will not be an operations man, he will not be a trust man. He will be a businessman, heavily impregnated with a fiduciary awareness."

Harvie's retirement dinners.

Top: State-Planters; Speakers Lewis F. Powell, Jr. (left) and Joseph A. Jennings.

Bottom right: United Virginia Bankshares; Presenting Harvie with the Steuben glass owl is Clarence J. Robinson.

From Harvie's perspective, the key to the future of any corporate organization resided in the quality of its executive personnel. "I have come [to decide] that it is far more difficult to find good management than it is to find capital," he once told a reporter. "You may have great need for your product and you may have adequacy of finance, but unless you have the managerial horses, the show will not stay on the road. Management is in greater deficit than is capital."

Upon Harvie's retirement from United Virginia Bankshares, tributes to the banker and the man poured into Richmond from across the state. Perhaps the most moving testimonial came from Harvie's oldest and closest friend, Lewis F. Powell, Jr. After acknowledging that Harvie had single-handedly "led Virginia banking out of its narrow and historic mold of unit banking," thereby transforming utterly the nature of financial affairs in the Commonwealth, Powell enumerated Wilkinson's "extraordinary contribution to education," including his service to the University of Virginia, the Richmond School Board, and Hollins College, which had granted him an honorary L.L.D. degree, one of the first to be awarded. Yet above all else, Powell praised the personal qualities of his longtime friend:

> He has exemplified the virtues — now being denigrated and ridiculed — of intense loyalty and devotion to friends, to the institutions with which he has been and is associated, and above all to this state and country. In short, Harvie's notable career is to be measured more by the intangibles of heart and spirit than by the truly impressive list of offices held, of board and of recorded achievements.

At his Bankshares retirement dinner — where he received a gift of a giant Steuben glass owl, the wise "bird of the night" with which Harvie had always been identified by his friends and colleagues — Harvie himself looked back at his career with considerable affection and expressed a hope for the future. "I have felt since my youth that I owe it to the society that received me and gave me my environment for life," he said, "to be a participant in the shaping — and now I quote Jefferson — 'of not what was to perish with me, but what would remain, be respected, and preserved through other ages.'"

There were those who predicted that Harvie Wilkinson would not be happy in retirement, that he would miss the constant challenge of directing Virginia's leading financial institution through the trials of an increasingly competitive business world. Indeed, in an attempt to cheer her husband and keep him busy, Letitia had arranged a trip to Savannah and Charleston for the two of them — and thence to Europe with the Sacketts — to begin two days after the last of Harvie's retirement parties.

But when the moment arrived, Harvie was perfectly willing to lay down at last the reins of power and responsibility. "When the holding company was in place," recalled Jay Wilkinson, "I think he had accomplished much of what he wanted. I think he was very relieved to see the day-to-day administrative responsibility turned over, the hundreds of small decisions that inevitably land on an administrator's desk." Harvie himself said as much on at least one occasion. "You have no idea," he told his younger son, Lewis, "how good it feels to have the yoke of responsibility lifted from around your neck."

Certainly Harvie now had more time to devote to his other intellectual pursuits. Always a prodigious reader of serious non-fiction — especially history, economics, and philosophy — Harvie also enjoyed Ian Fleming thrillers and Rex Stout's "Nero Wolfe" mysteries (perhaps because Wolfe was a renowned gourmet). As his eyesight began to fail, Harvie found himself turning to television to obtain his daily news reports; in fact, Letitia recalled that "if the phone rang between 6:30 and 7:00, when the evening news was on, the rule at the house was that we do not answer it." And friends soon learned never to invite Harvie to dinner until after seven o'clock.

Doubtless Harvie was gratified by the resurgence of the Washington Redskins under head coach George Allen in the early 1970s, and he especially enjoyed watching star quarterback Sonny Jurgensen, whose gridiron talents were rivaled only by his love of the good life off the field. Aside from sports, the news, and documentaries, Harvie's tastes in television were certainly eclectic if nothing else, as he became a loyal fan of such diverse programs as the western "Gunsmoke," "Masterpiece Theater," and "The Cosby Show."

Although he accepted the board of directors' offer to remain with the bank in an advisory capacity, as chairman of the Finance Committee of United Virginia Bankshares and a director of Capitoline Investment Services (the bank's investment counseling and management subsidiary), Harvie realized that the holding company had grown far too large to be directed by a single individual. There would be no more Harvie Wilkinsons in the future of Virginia banking.

Harvie upon the occasion of his retirement from the Board
of Trustees of Colonial Williamsburg in 1976. Presenting
the gift is Lewis F. Powell, Jr.

For Harvie, retirement represented a chance to indulge his broad-gauged interests outside of the banking world, and to inaugurate another career in public service. Since 1968, Harvie had been a member of the Board of Trustees of Colonial Williamsburg, Inc., and a director of Williamsburg Restoration, Inc. Now he was able to dedicate even more time to this cause so dear to his heart, contributing his financial expertise to an organization vitally concerned with the preservation — and education — of the history and tradition of Virginia.

Harvie also remained active in the political administration of his native city. In the winter of 1972, slightly more than six months after his retirement, he agreed to serve as chairman of a search committee to recommend a new city manager for Richmond. In discussing his committee's criteria for a nominee, Harvie explained that "anyone who

Ross R. Millhiser, Vice-Chairman, Board of Directors, Philip Morris, Incorporated, New York, presents a check for the first installment on the company's $500,000 challenge gift to the Virginia Museum Endowment Campaign in the spring of 1981.

Left to right: Charles L. Reed, Jr., President, Virginia Museum, Ross Millhiser, T. Justin Moore, Chairman, VEPCO and J. Harvie Wilkinson, Jr., Vice Chairman of the Endowment Campaign.

comes here has to be able to deal biracially with equity and forthrightness, and he has to be familiar with such issues as revenue sharing and intergovernmental relationships. We must have a man with broad experience and the capacity to relate to the many facets of city government — engineering, financial, recreation, personnel matters, and so forth. Actually," he concluded, "it sounds like we are looking for a chap among the angelic hosts who might come to the job" — or someone who shared Harvie's own commitment and dedication to city government.

In June 1972, Wilkinson accepted an appointment by Governor Linwood Holton to the Board of Trustees of the Virginia Museum of Fine Arts. For the next decade, Harvie made the Museum one of his primary concerns, serving as chairman of its Development, Finance, and Education in the Arts Committees, and as vice president of the board from 1974 to 1978. Besides contributing his fund-raising abilities and statewide contacts to the Museum, Harvie was able to work with the Museum staff to review its

William K. Klingaman received a Ph.D. in American history from the University of Virginia in 1978 and is a specialist in twentieth-century American affairs. He has served as a historical consultant to the Under Secretary of Defense and co-edited the Department of State's *Foreign Relations Of The United States* series. Dr. Klingaman has taught at the University of Virginia, and currently is a member of the faculty at the University of Maryland.

He is the author of a trilogy on twentieth century history:

1919: The Year Our World Began (St. Martin's Press, 1987).
1941: Our Lives In A World On The Edge (Harper & Row, 1988).
1929: The Year Of The Great Crash (Harper & Row, 1989).

His other works include the following:

APL—Fifty Years Of Service To The Nation (The Johns Hopkins University Applied Physics Laboratory, 1993).
GEICO: The First Forty Years (1994).
The First Century: Emperors, Gods And Everyman (HarperCollins, 1990).
Turning 40 (NAL/Dutton, 1992).
Turning 50 (NAL/Dutton, 1994).

Dr. Klingaman also has a forthcoming book, due out in early 1995, titled *The McCarthy Era*.

He resides in Columbia, Maryland, with his wife, Janet and two children.